CREDENTIALING IN COUNSELING

EDITED BY FRED O. BRADLEY

Association for Couns
Supervision and Educ
5999 Stevenson Ave
Alexandria, VA 223

Copyright © 1991 by the American Association for Counseling and Development
(AACD became the American Counseling Association on July 1, 1992)

American Counseling Association
5999 Stevenson Avenue
Alexandria, VA 22304

Cover Design by Sarah Jane Valdez

LC catalog card number 91-15098
Cataloging-in-Publication Data is available.
ISBN 1-55620-087-0

Printed in the United States of America

Contents

Preface v
Michael K. Altekruse

Introduction ix
Fred O. Bradley

CHAPTER 1   Counselor Credentialing: Purpose and Origin 1
Thomas J. Sweeney

CHAPTER 2   Counselor Certification 13
Donald V. Forrest and Lloyd A. Stone

CHAPTER 3   Historical Antecedents and Current Status of
Counselor Licensure 23
Thomas W. Hosie

CHAPTER 4   Accreditation in Counselor Education 53
Michael K. Altekruse and Joe Wittmer

CHAPTER 5   A View From the Profession: What We Think of
Where We Are? 63
Donald C. Waterstreet

CHAPTER 6   Concerns About Accreditation and Credentialing:
A Personal View 69
Kenneth B. Hoyt

CHAPTER 7   An Argument for Credentialing 81
Theodore P. Remley

APPENDIX A   A Summary of Counselor Credentialing Legislation ... 86
Carol S. Vroman and John W. Bloom

APPENDIX B   Professional Certifying Bodies 103

APPENDIX C   CACREP-Approved Programs 105

APPENDIX D   CACREP Accreditation Process 110

Preface

When one is chosen president elect-elect of the Association for Counselor Education and Supervision (ACES), an early task is to select a theme for his or her year as president. My long dedication to accreditation in counseling, the current activity to modify the Council for Accreditation for Counseling and Related Educational Programs (CACREP) standards, the strong movement toward professional counselor licensure sweeping the country, and the overwhelming support for professional certification all led to the selection of a credentialing theme for my period as president of ACES.

Credentialing in all forms became a priority for the American Association for Counseling and Development (AACD), then the American Personnel and Guidance Association (APGA), in the 1970s. ACES was an early leader in the credentialing movement and was the first national professional association associated with APGA to accredit training programs. In the recent past, as well as the present, many ACES members have felt that it was time to reevaluate the credentialing movement in counseling and consider plans for the future. Thus, the ACES theme for 1990–1991, "Credentialing Revisited," was created.

During the 1990–1991 year, the ACES members attending the regional meetings were surveyed on various aspects of credentialing, the CACREP standards were extensively reviewed, and the theme of credentialing was chosen as the focus of this 1991 ACES monograph. Present and past leaders in the credentialing movement were chosen to share with you the history and future of credentialing. This monograph is another in a series of ACES publications that can serve as a valuable resource for counselors, counselor trainees, counselor supervisors, and counselor educators.

Michael K. Altekruse, EdD
1989–1990 ACES President

Contributors

Michael K. Altekruse is the 1989–1990 president of ACES and professor and program coordinator, counselor education, Department of Educational Psychology, School of Education, Southern Illinois University-Carbondale.

John W. Bloom is chairperson of the AACD Licensure Committee and professor, Department of Counselor Education, College of Education, University of Northern Arizona.

Fred O. Bradley was the 1986–1987 president of NCACES and is presently professor, Department of Counseling and Educational Psychology, College of Education, Kansas State University.

Donald V. Forrest is the 1990–1991 president of RMACES and professor, Department of Counselor Education, College of Education, University of Wyoming.

Thomas W. Hosie was the 1989–1990 president of ACES and is professor and program coordinator, counselor education, Louisiana State University.

Kenneth B. Hoyt was the 1966–1967 president of APGA and presently is university distinguished professor of education, Kansas State University.

Theodore P. Remley is executive director of AACD.

Lloyd A. Stone is the 1990–1991 president of NCACES and professor and department head, Counselor Education and Rehabilitation Programs, Emporia State University.

Thomas J. Sweeney was 1976–1977 president of ACES and is professor and chairperson, counselor education, College of Education, University of Ohio.

Carol S. Vroman is chair of the Counseling Credentialing Committee of the Arizona Board of Behavioral Health Examiners and a counselor in private practice in Phoenix, Arizona.

Donald C. Waterstreet was the 1977–1978 president of NCACES and is presently professor and department chair, counselor education, School of Education, Western Illinois University.

Joe Wittmer is the former executive director of CACREP and professor, counselor education, University of Florida.

Introduction

Fred O. Bradley

This brief introduction provides an orientation to this monograph on credentialing and the manner in which the various aspects of this important topic are addressed. The monograph is organized to discuss all aspects of credentialing from both a past and present perspective, to consider the future of counselor credentialing, and to provide a synopsis of the credentialing movement in counseling. The material contained in this publication represents a current view of the status of counselor credentialing in the United States and presents the collective efforts of a group of individuals who have been active, if not instrumental, in various facets of the overall credentialing movement.

Without question, counselor credentialing is the topic of the day. Moreover, credentialing is a fundamental part of the growth and development of any profession, and because counseling is a relatively young field, the advances that have been made in becoming a profession can be clearly associated with the credentialing activity that has taken place in the past two decades. Nevertheless, even though the growth of the field has been expansive over the past decade, exceeding that of prior decades, counseling is still regarded as a neophyte when compared to some of the other helping professions. Many of the leaders in the field believe that the key to continued growth in counseling is the credentialing movement.

The term *credentialing* is a coined word that represents the broad spectrum of efforts surrounding the establishment of professional training standards and regulations for practice. The credentialing movement has by no means been isolated to counseling. By varying degrees, similar efforts have been under way in psychology, social work, marriage and family therapy, rehabilitation counseling, alcohol and drug counseling, and other helping professions. Among these fields psychology has been the leader, with social work and counseling following closely behind. The development of professional training and practice standards is a much older movement, originating during the Middle Ages. Chapter 4 indicates how the medical profession and the guilds, forerunners to professional societies, provided the early leadership in the development of training standards and the regulation of professions.

The particular areas considered under the general rubric of credentialing are licensure, registry, and accreditation. Licensure is an effort of state government to regulate professions. This effort includes registration/certification—protection of title and licensing—protection of practice. The summary of legislation provided in appendix A clearly outlines the various forms of counselor licensing acts. When this summary is reviewed, it is readily apparent that most laws are *title* acts rather than *practice* acts. What is generally not recognized by counselors who are impatient to obtain full fledged licensure is that psychologists in many states started with title legislation.

Another term used in connection with legislative credentialing is *certification*. This term is confusing because it is used on some occasions to represent legislatively initiated title regulation and on other occasions to refer to practice regulation. Also, certification is used to represent school counselor credentialing by state departments of education.

Registry is a process by an organization or agency to identify training and experience requirements of members of a professional group. Those individuals who are identified as having met the necessary requirements are listed in a publication generally called a registry. Registry should not be confused with registration, which is a legislatively initiated titular credential. One of the early registry bodies was the National Register of Health Service Providers in Psychology, which endeavored to provide a national listing of qualified psychologists. In the counseling profession, the National Board for Certified Counselors (NBCC) is the primary registry body.

Accreditation is a process of approving formal training programs. Accrediting bodies usually have been formed through professional organizations to prescribe the curricula and experiences for the training of a group of professionals.

The broad definitions provided above are intended to help readers focus their attention on the area or particular form of credentialing under discussion. An overview of each of the chapters and the way each addresses credentialing follows.

Chapter 1 looks at the total credentialing movement and provides historical evidence to give a foundation for subsequent activity. The chapter, which addresses the broad spectrum rather than individual aspects of credentialing, first describes the various forms of credentialing, dividing them into registry, certification, and licensure. The author, Thomas J. Sweeney, then discusses counselor credentialing, tracing the historical development of each form, including school counseling, rehabilitation counseling, mental health counseling, the National Board for Certified Counselors, and licensure. The chapter concludes with a consideration of the immediate needs in the credentialing movement.

Chapter 2 covers counselor certification. Authors Donald V. Forrest and Lloyd A. Stone regard certification as including all nonstatutory efforts by associations or governmental agencies to provide recognition to individuals who have met identified professional qualifications. They first enumerate the benefits of certification and then proceed to discuss certification by describing various registries. Next, they outline a chronology of counselor certification, showing the evolution from school counseling certification to the recently added career counselor certification, as a speciality within NBCC. Their conclusion provides observations regarding the possible collaborative efforts between NBCC and state departments of education to certify counselors.

In chapter 3 author Thomas W. Hosie comprehensively reviews licensure as the efforts of state governments to provide statutory regulation of counselors. He discusses the history of licensing and professional regulation and through his historical discussion sketches the development of a profession. Further, he provides a critique of legislated credentialing that brings into perspective the pros and cons of regulation. Other forms of credentialing are also addressed to support the primary discussion of licensure. To complement the material on licensure in chapter 3, compilers Carol S. Vroman and John W. Bloom provide a complete and up-to-date summary of counselor credentialing legislation in appendix A. These two elements of this monograph will prove invaluable to readers desiring a historical perspective as well as a current understanding of the licensure activity in counseling.

Chapter 4 not only traces the developmental process of counselor accreditation but also highlights accreditation in other helping professions. Authors Michael K. Altekruse and Joe Wittmer bring their extensive experience in the accreditation movement to bear here. The primary focus is the evolution of CACREP and its current status. Because CACREP is the primary accreditation effort undertaken in the counseling profession, this chapter provides an extensive examination of the standards.

The survey of ACES members who attended the 1989 regional ACES conventions is the focus of chapter 5. This survey was one of the tasks undertaken by a committee created by Michael K. Altekruse when he became president-elect of ACES. The committee was constituted to represent a cross section of individuals and credentialing bodies in AACD and ACES. The members of this committee were Donald C. Waterstreet, Robert E. Comas, Bree A. Hayes, Donald V. Forrest, Michael K. Altekruse, and Robert L. Frank. The data from this survey represented the views of approximately 228 members of ACES in attendance at the conventions. The data are summarized and briefly discussed by author Donald C. Waterstreet. Also included in the chapter are recommendations of the committee.

Chapter 6 provides a view of credentialing from the perspective of an individual long in the field and well known for his reservations about credentialing efforts and for his forthright views. Author Kenneth B. Hoyt's analysis of accreditation and his discussion of his concerns about the whole credentialing effort are "food for thought."

Chapter 7 draws a proactive conclusion to this monograph. Author Theodore P. Remley, who is AACD's current executive director, summarizes the arguments for and against credentialing and concludes that credentialing's positive effects substantially outweigh any negative arguments.

The four appendices are included as supplements to the text. In some cases specific references are made to this supporting information (as already the case for appendix A). In other cases the appendix material was selected to serve as a general complement to the text material and needs no specific citation.

A final note: The contributors to this monograph represent only a few of the many individuals who have been active in the credentialing movement. Each of the authors has attempted to credit those who have labored to bring our profession to its present status. The absence of recognition to any particular individual is unintentional.

CHAPTER 1

Counselor Credentialing: Purpose and Origin

Thomas J. Sweeney

Credentialing in the counseling profession is no longer a new subject. This has not been the case, however, in the recent past (Sweeney & Sturdevant, 1974). Through the sometimes harsh realities of court decisions or licensing board actions, counselors learned that credentialing was a marketplace fact of life (Sweeney, 1978a, 1978b; Sweeney & Witmer, 1977). Today, with circumstances changing again, credentialing needs to be reconceptualized in order for counselors to anticipate future implications of these symbols of credibility for practice.

This chapter is designed to place credentialing methods into a broader context and within a historical perspective, and to provide an overview, rather than an in-depth exposition of each method, with the intention of providing a context for the chapters that follow. Although both national and state certification are available to counselors, they are neither well articulated nor comparable. What serves some counselors is not as useful for others. Counselors have been slow to respond to changing marketplace issues. Now that we are more conscious of such issues, we must be intelligent in our responses.

Knowledge of credentialing in the past, therefore, can be useful in preparing plans for the future. Understanding the similarities and differences among credentialing methods is a first step.

Purpose and Types of Credentials

Credentialing involves at least three methods, with variations on each. These include registry, certification, and licensure. Each of these deserves some explanation of differences, including advantages and disadvantages in relation to their place in counselor credentialing.

Registry, in its simplest form, is a voluntary listing of individuals who use a title and/or provide a service for which a government or occupational group believes that it is of benefit to require or encourage registration. Generally, the criteria for inclusion are met by the least restrictive methods

1

used in the three different credentialing strategies. Cost for inclusion, therefore, can be relatively modest. Usually there is no effort to regulate practitioners or the practice by others not so registered. Renewal is automatic upon payment of specified maintenance fees. Although it may seem to be the least desirable method for professional occupations, it does have its place and is of interest to counselors.

To certify is "to vouch for the truth of" by Webster's definition (Allee, 1984). Certification, therefore, is broadly conceived as a process of verifying the truth of one's assertion of qualification, in our case, as professional counselors. School counselors have been certified in all states by some mechanism for more than two decades. Certification, unlike licensure, can be established by other than state law. Most counselors are familiar with nonlegislative certification as established, for example, by the National Board for Certified Counselors. There are significant differences in these two forms of certification, however.

State legislatures or other governmental agencies authorized by them, such as departments of education or mental health, establish criteria and methods for certification that they consider appropriate for their state and its needs. As a consequence, the standards agreed upon by an occupational group represented, for example, by AACD and its accrediting body (CACREP), may be considered—or totally disregarded—in any such credentialing. This has led to much difficulty in establishing reciprocity among state certifying bodies and has deflected efforts to promote counseling as a unique profession whose practitioners possess specific knowledge and skills.

Profession-promulgated national certification, by contrast, can promote counseling as a distinct profession through uniformity in its criteria for certification as a counselor. It may establish additional criteria for renewal of certification and for specialization within the field beyond the entry-level criteria. It commonly promotes continuing education of its participants and requires strict adherence to a professional code of conduct. Its chief disadvantage lies in the fact that it has no authority beyond determining who meets the criteria and who may be retained or renewed as a counselor. Adherence to these standards for any other purpose by any other agency, employer, or person is totally voluntary. Likewise, noncertificated persons may practice without regard to the preparation standards or code of ethics.

Licensure is another legislatively established basis of credentialing. It tends to be the most desirable with respect to asserting the uniqueness of an occupation because it may delimit both the title and practice of an occupation.

One caveat is appropriate at this juncture. In any given state, registry, certification, or licensure may or may not have the characteristics as presented in this chapter. These characteristics are generally accurate, but each state legislature may modify them to suit its own purposes. Therefore, a certificate in one state may be administered like a registration in another state. Only by examining a specific law and the rules by which it is administered can one determine the full implications of the law in that state. To refer to licensing laws as though they were similar in any other way than by title can be both misleading and inaccurate. In fact, some state laws for licensing counselors are more accurately descriptive of a certification or registry process.

Counselor Credentialing: How and When

School Counseling

School counselor certification received its greatest impetus from the implementation of the National Defense Education Act of 1958. Thousands of educators were trained and hired to work in schools as counselors. Their mission, according to Congress, was to identify and guide the mathematically and scientifically talented youth of our country to pursue curricula and careers in technical and scientific fields for the benefit of a national effort to overcome a perceived deficit in our race with the Soviet Union to space. The need for state departments of education to establish criteria that would qualify schools to receive federal funds for the services of these personnel was a compelling reason behind the rapid growth of certification. This was especially true for states that had had little motivation to distinguish counselors from teachers before this time.

Counseling personnel seized upon this opportunity to help influence such state legislation. Early efforts by the American School Counselors Association (ASCA) and the Association for Counselor Education and Supervision (Stripling, 1965) to establish national standards ultimately became the template for all counselor preparation standards under the aegis of AACD. Uniformity in certification criteria among states was still a problem for the reasons already noted with differences in legislatures. This was further compounded by the lack of a national counseling accrediting body to implement the agreed-upon standards.

Without a national accreditation body, counselor education programs of the 1960s and 1970s could not use the standards effectively with their college deans and university curricular committees to win support for subscribing to them. In fact, there were counselor educators (Stripling, 1979) who proposed that all counselor education accreditation be conducted by the National Council for Accreditation of Teacher Education (NCATE) rather than risking failure with a new, separate accrediting body such as CACREP. Naturally, this point of view was embraced by many college deans and presidents who inherently oppose any new accrediting bodies. Ultimately, such persuasion was overcome by the reality that NCATE was neither interested in nor capable of assuming responsibility for the accreditation of yet another discipline. Nevertheless, the lack of unanimity on purpose and goals even among counselor educators did little to advance the professionalization of counseling.

With the funding challenges facing schools, school counselor positions in the 1980s were stable or declining with a few notable exceptions, especially in elementary school counseling, which had an upsurge in some states. As a consequence, school counselor certification did not progress and, in some cases, has been eroded by educators and boards of education members' responses to criticism of education, in general, and teacher competencies, in particular. In Ohio, for example, teacher certification was changed to emphasize graduate degrees in subject areas for continuing certification. At the same time, the state board of education changed school standards such that counselor-pupil ratios are no longer required and bachelor's degree social workers can be hired to do pupil personnel work in the schools. Unfortunately, there has been insufficient attention to this area of credentialing in the last decade (Sweeney, 1988).

Rehabilitation Counseling

Rehabilitation counselor certification was the first such national credentialing, with its establishment in 1973 (Livingston, 1979). The Commission on Rehabilitation Counselor Certification (CRCC) has administered its examination to more than 12,000 individuals since that time. Its efforts have been furthered, to some extent, by the fact that a national accreditation body, the Council for Rehabilitation Education (CORE), developed national standards and a unique program review process that helped preparation programs align their curricula to the national standards.

Unfortunately, state rehabilitation agency policies and legislation funding rehabilitation services have not followed recommendations for full implementation of the national standards. As a consequence, both agency and private service providers are able to fill positions with less than a Certified Rehabilitation Counselor (CRC).

Mental Health Counseling

The National Academy of Certified Clinical Mental Health Counselors (NACCMHC) was our next national certifying body. Since its inception in 1979, the academy has certified approximately 1,400 individuals. Through aggressive and persistent lobbying, the academy and its parent body, the American Mental Health Counselors Association (AMHCA), have earned recognition for these certificate holders by the Civilian Health and Medical Program of the Uniformed Services (CHAMPUS) as meeting standards for third-party payment with a physician's referral.

CHAMPUS recognition is an important step in helping to put qualified counselors in a more competitive position with other mental health providers of these services. Unfortunately, the relatively small number of individuals certificated works to the detriment of efforts to gain more widespread recognition for those so certified in some quarters. With more than two-thirds of the states now providing some form of credentialing for counselors, these counselors seem not disposed to seek yet another credential unless it can be linked to income or mobility enhancement. Third-party reimbursement is one such issue.

The marketplace issue of third-party payment is a concern to all insurance agencies, governmental and private. As a consequence, managed health care proposals are coming forth to contain costs. One strategy is to limit who can provide services. Medical organizations, including those of psychiatrists, wish to limit nonmedical personnel. As more evidence indicates that preventative and early intervention by nonmedical programs are effective, these efforts can be thwarted (Hosie, West, & Mackey, 1988, 1990; Winslow, 1989). In the meantime, however, counselors must be more cognizant of the implications of health management organizations (HMOs) and preferred provider organizations (PPOs) for future practice.

Liability for negligence or improper care are major issues to all service providers. Likewise, cost containment motivates changes to the health care delivery system. These are of such a magnitude, of such a compelling nature, that to make a place and survive in this market, counselors must be prepared to speak the language and offer a coherent voice to the solutions or we simply will be seen as a part of the problem. For those counselors now and in the future who desire to work in the health care delivery system, there is an imperative to pursue a clear, articulate plan in which our credentialing efforts are a central component.

National Board for Certified Counselors

Perhaps the most visible and certainly the largest national certifying body is the National Board for Certified Counselors. Established by AACD/APGA in 1981 as a free-standing corporate body, it now has certified over 17,000 counselors in this country and Europe (Americans overseas). Interestingly, the AACD/APGA Governing Council was proposing to discontinue what had been known as its Registry Committee when the author and the chair of the committee, Lloyd A. Stone, developed a survey for distribution to a 10% random sample of the membership. The response was the most immediate and largest in the association's history. Based upon the members' response, NBCC became a priority and, shortly thereafter, a reality.

NBCC has since established three additional specialty certifications. The first, the National Certified Career Counselor (NCCC), was established by the National Career Development Association (NCDA) in response to its perception that the public needs access to qualified career counselors. The validity of this position has been corroborated by NBCC headquarters staff who report that they have received 10 times as many requests for certified counselors than are available. This demand has not reached the counselors, however, as only 1,000 or so have sought this additional specialty certification.

NBCC Specialties

The newest specialties come from one of the oldest and one of newest divisions of AACD. The leaders of ASCA were encouraged by the NBCC to establish a committee and submit a proposal to create a National Certified School Counselor (NCSC) specialty. This is being implemented in 1991 and is another important component of a credentialing plan to create greater uniformity in school counselor certification in the states and to promote these standards for federally and state-funded pupil personnel programs in the future.

AACD has conducted for many years projects funded by the U.S. Administration on Aging and related volunteer projects. As a result, the NBCC was petitioned by project director Jane Myers (personal correspondence, January 1990) to establish a specialization in gerontological counseling. The multiyear projects had compiled data demonstrating a need, created curricular guides and video resource materials, established nationally derived entry-level and specialty competencies, and outlined possible preparation standards. With the full participation and endorsement of the Association for Adult Development and Aging (AADA) leaders, the NBCC accepted the proposal and has established the criteria for this specialization, which is also being implemented in 1991.

Licensure

Licensure has been the major focus of AACD's credentialing efforts since the mid-1970s. In 1973, the author presented a paper at the Southern Association for Counselor Education and Supervision (SACES), which resulted in his chairing the SACES Committee on Licensure, the first for the profession. (This paper was subsequently published—see Sweeney & Sturdevant, 1974.) Next came preparing the AACD/APGA-adopted policy, *Counselor Licensure: Position Statement*, and chairing its commission to implement a policy "in favor of vigorous, responsible action to establish provisions for the licensure of professional counselors in the various states" (APGA, 1974). There are currently 34 states with regulations on the practice of professional counseling. Most of these are licensing laws. A short overview of this history is important.

The profession of psychology began in the 1940s to be concerned about the image and status of psychology among other professions and the public. One of these efforts was to turn to state legislatures. The first laws for psychologists were passed in Connecticut (1945) and Virginia (1946). But in the 10-year period from 1945 to 1954, only seven states passed licensing or certification laws. In the next 10-year period ending in 1964, 18 additional states passed legislation (Little, 1973). Psychologists also discovered the practical differences among the forms of credentialing. Unhappily, what some promoters found was that persons could still practice without a certificate. What had been gained was not sufficient. A new study was done. A report of the American Psychological Association (APA) Committee on Legislation (APA, 1967) became the guidelines for the formation of new, more definitive licensing law language.

Various state psychology groups began acting on these recommendations. One result in Virginia was the cease-and-desist order to a counselor in private practice in *Weldon v. Virginia State Board of Psychologist Examiners* (1972). The court ruled that Weldon was practicing outside of the law but that the Virginia legislature had created the problem by violating his right to practice his profession (which the court ruled to be separate from psychology). As a consequence, the first legislation for professional counselors was passed by the Virginia legislature in its next session.

Ohio was one of the first states that followed the APA committee recommendations closely and incorporated them successfully into a licensing law. The first board enthusiastically went to work with a goal of delimiting the practice of psychology. The problems for counselors began with the definition of psychology:

> The practice of psychology . . . is defined as rendering to individuals, groups, and organizations or the public any psychological services involving the application of principles, methods, and procedures of understanding, predicting, and influencing behavior, such as pertaining to learning, perception, motivation, thinking, emotions, and interpersonal relationships; the methods and procedures of interviewing, counseling, and psychotherapy; constructing, administering, and interpreting tests of mental abilities; aptitude, interests, attitudes, personality characteristics, emotion, and motivation; and of assessing public opinion. (APA, 1967, p. 1099)

It is obvious that any other unregulated occupation involving human services is included in this definition.

The second factor that distinguished licensure from other credentials, however, became equally problematic. Boards are empowered to generate rules for the implementation of the law. In Ohio, at one time, the board sent a notice to the presidents of all institutions of higher educaiton stating that anyone who taught courses of a psychological nature should be licensed or license eligible. Hundreds of teachers in various university and college departments were to be required to demonstrate compliance. This notice had to be rescinded because some institutions took exception to the board's action, but it reflects the zeal of that board in its efforts to establish its authority.

In the case of the *City of Cleveland, Ohio v. Cook* (1975), Cook was arrested on a felony and sued for practicing psychology without a license. Cook, well known and respected in his community, was employed at a 2-year college and provided private school testing assessment part time. He did not refer to himself as a psychologist, but he titled his reports as psychological evaluations. He was properly educated and qualified to offer these services as a counselor. He had written to the board requesting information about licensure twice, but before he received an answer, he was booked at the local police station. The Cleveland newspaper reported the incident, and his reputation was immediately tarnished.

Cook was an APGA member, and he and his attorney received immediate consultation through the author. Carl Swanson, an attorney and counselor educator who co-chaired the APGA Licensure Committee at that time, offered supporting testimony at his trial. In a directed verdict, the court found Cook not guilty, but the damage to his practice and reputation already were done. This is but one of numerous instances of such problems. The AACD Legal Defense Fund is an outgrowth of these kinds of cases.

Equally damaging are the many instances when administrative rules specifying that only licensed or certified practitioners can be employed are implemented by state and federal agencies. These same rules often specify as well that only the licensed persons may supervise psychological services. In the late 1970s, an agency in the state of Alabama eliminated all counselor position titles for the entire state because of such thinking.

Many university counseling centers will hire only psychologists, while others specify that only psychologists can supervise and direct their centers. These practices were, and to some extent still are, reinforced by the standards of the AACD affiliate organization, the International Accreditation of Counseling Services (IACS). Until the early 1980s, these standards were worded to give psychologists preferences over "other related fields." Currently, they give preference to psychologists as the directors of such centers. There are indications that the next edition of these standards may correct this bias.

Although there are many other such examples as those given above, the circumstances motivating the initial licensure effort of AACD were tied closely to the rights of counselors to practice and of their clients to have access to their services. We still are moving toward similar goals, but the counselors' position is significantly more secure because of the efforts of hundreds of persons in virtually every state. But getting licensure laws passed, certifications established, and national accreditation implemented is only the beginning of what is needed.

Credentialing: What Now?

Credentialing and accreditation are cornerstones for the counseling profession's future efforts to gain equity in the marketplace. Although we have pursued each with "vigor," the vision of what we are working for has not been well articulated. At the present time, the differences among views of what we are attempting to achieve may be no less than the differences in points of view with other professions (Gerstein & Brooks, 1990).

What is needed now is a common view and a mechanism for coordinating these major activities. AACD has reaffirmed "professionalization" activities as a major priority. A new organizational structure has been implemented to coordinate the activities of the association while facilitating the opportunity for dialogue among its various sibling organizations. This well may be the mechanism not only for developing a common vision but also for furthering its realization. Credentialing bodies (NBCC, NACCMHC, association of state licensing boards) and accreditation agencies (CACREP and IACS) can be augmented by AACD and its divisions' committees on professional advocacy, government relations, ethics, and related topics. A historic meeting of all these groups in the fall of 1990 with AACD leaders, committee chairs, division representatives, and interested observers resulted in many agreements on goals and objectives for professionalization. These are to be reviewed and revised periodically under the guidance and with the approval of the AACD Governing Council.

The goals and objectives will no doubt address the following needs if counseling professionalization is to accelerate. These include:

1. a philosophical position that each AACD or affiliate credentialing activity will be encouraged in its efforts to further the profession of counseling
2. a national effort through the Public Health Services Act of 1973 to include counseling as a discipline among the core providers of services
3. a two-pronged effort in licensure and state certification (a) to establish greater uniformity among state legislation in keeping with national certification and preparation standards and (b) to pass legislation in states without legislation by providing intensive support to the counselors in those states
4. professional advocacy, starting within AACD, to insure that its constituent organizations are in concert with the association's strategic goals, and with state and federal agencies whose bureaucratic rules and regulations discriminate against or otherwise impede career development for counselors
5. at least one nationally accredited counselor preparation program in every state and more where preparation programs are in greater numbers

6. national and state credentialing examinations and accreditation standards that emphasize clinical performance and outcome measures of competence.

There are many more issues related to professionalization and credentialing that deserve attention. Interprofessional rivalry is alive but not well, i.e., not healthy for the profession (Gerstein & Brooks, 1990). Among psychiatrists, psychologists, social workers, counselors, and marriage and family therapists, the turf issues only exacerbate the challenges to each in delivering effective services to the public. Even within AACD, Brooks and Gerstein (1990) hold the opinion that AACD's recognition of its newest and fastest growing division, the International Association for Marriage and Family Counselors (IAMFC), can be construed as showing bad faith to the American Association of Marriage and Family Therapy (AAMFT). This may more accurately reflect myopic vision of the authors' than of AACD's Governing Council, however.

What few members know is that efforts were made in the late 1970s and early 1980s to encourage the AAMFT to consider joining APGA, or at least work more closely together on licensure and accreditation activities. As one involved in both formal and informal contacts with AAMFT leaders, the author knows that we owe no apologies to anyone on our sincerity or openness to dialogue. The AAMFT leadership at that time chose to maintain a distance from counselors. This seemed true in part because the organization had only dropped its identification with counseling in its title a few years earlier.

Had AAMFT entertained these overtures, how different our licensure laws and national standards might be today. How different AAMFT might be today. By its rapid and substantial growth, our newest division shows it is clearly filling a need long overdue. It is pointless to lament or blame others for our individual or collective lack of full collaboration.

Our rehabilitation credentialing and accreditation bodies, CRCC and CORE, must wonder where AACD's efforts will take the professions in the future. Hopefully, they will be interested in participating in the dialogues that will be going on to answer these questions.

Conclusion

Credentialing may be seen as a "many splendored thing," as a myriad of activities sometimes opposing one another, sometimes complementing one another. Something of both is currently true. The optimist will say that we are half way toward our original goal. The pessimist may say that we have not gone far enough, and that is bad. What is worse is to believe that we will never truly achieve our goals. As subsequent chapters will reveal, we are well on our way. The question is not "Will we attain our goals?" but "When?"!

References

Allee, J.G. (Ed.). (1984). *Webster's Dictionary*. Baltimore, MD: Harbor House.

American Personnel and Guidance Association. (1974, July). Counselor Licensure: Position Statement. Adopted by American Personnel and Guidance Association Governing Council. Washington, DC: Author.

American Psychological Association. (1967). A model for state legislation affecting the practice of psychology. 1967: A report of APA Committee on Legislation. *American Psychologist, 22*(12), 1095–1103.

Brooks, D.K., Jr., & Gerstein, L.H. (1990). Interprofessional collaboration: Or shooting yourself in the foot only feels good when you stop. *Counseling and Development Journal, 68*(5), 509–510.

City of Cleveland, Ohio v. Cook, Municipal Court, Criminal Division, No. 75-CRB 11478, August 12, 1975. (Transcript dated August 19, 1975).

Gerstein, L.H., & Brooks, D.K., Jr. (1990). The helping professions' challenge: Credentialing and interdisciplinary collaboration. *Journal of Counseling and Development, 68*(5), 475–523.

Hosie, T.W., West, J.D., & Mackey, J.A. (1988). Employment and roles of mental health counselors in substance abuse centers. *Journal of Mental Health Counseling, 10*(3), 188–198.

Hosie, T.W., West, J.D., & Mackey, J.A. (1990). Perceptions of counselor performance in substance abuse centers. *Journal of Mental Health Counseling, 12*(2), 198–206.

Little, K. (1973, October). *Licensure in the helping professions: Prospects and problems.* Paper presented at the meeting of the Southern Association for Counselor Education and Supervision, Gatlinburg, TN.

Livingston, R. (1979). The history of rehabilitation counselor certification. *Journal of Applied Rehabilitation Counseling, 10*, 111–118.

Stripling, R.O. (1965). Standards for the preparation of school counselors. In J. Loughary (Ed.), *Counseling: A growing profession.* Washington, DC: American Personnel and Guidance Association.

Stripling, R.O. (1979). Standards and accreditation: A proposal. *Personnel and Guidance Journal, 56*(10), 608–611.

Sweeney, T.J. (1978a). Counselor credentialing: Promises and pitfalls. *Viewpoints in Teaching and Learning, 54*(1), 56–63.

Sweeney, T.J. (1978b). Polemics: the struggle for credentialing. *Illinois Personnel and Guidance Quarterly, 70*, 19–25.

Sweeney, T.J. (1988). Building strong school counseling programs: Implications for counselor preparation. In G. Walz (Ed.), *Building strong school counseling programs* (pp. 155–168). Alexandria, VA: American Association for Counseling and Development.

Sweeney, T.J., & Sturdevant, A.D. (1974). Licensure in the helping professions: Anatomy of an issue. *Personnel and Guidance Journal, 52*(9), 575–580.

Sweeney, T.J., & Witmer, J.M. (1977). Who says you're a counselor? *Personnel and Guidance Journal, 55*, 589–594.

Weldon v. Virginia State Board of Psychologist Examiners. Corporation Court Opinion (Court Order), Newport News, VA, October 4, 1972.

Winslow, R. (1989, December 13). Spending to cut mental-health costs. *The Wall Street Journal*, p. B1.

CHAPTER 2

Counselor Certification

Donald V. Forrest and Lloyd A. Stone

A profession has two common methods of credentialing: certification and licensure. The purpose of this chapter is to explore the process of certification, particularly as it pertains to counselors. The chapter presents a definition of certification and includes a discussion of the expected benefits. Also included is a brief historical chronology and an outline of the requirements for generic and specialty certification of counselors. Finally, future projections for counselor certification and considerations for specialty expansion are discussed.

Certification is a process of recognizing the competence of practitioners of a profession by officially authorizing them to use the title adopted by the profession (Forster, 1977). Another description of certification is that it is a process by which the professional certifying board grants formal recognition to an individual who has met certain predetermined standards as specified by that group (Baruth & Robinson, 1987). It is sometimes referred to as "title control" because only those who have met the standard are entitled to use the designated title; however, licensure is also a title control process.

Certification can be awarded by voluntary associations, agencies, or government bodies based on specified skills. However, only in a few instances are noncertified individuals prevented from practicing the skills of those who are certified. For example, a teaching certificate is generally required to teach in a public school but not in other settings. Certification is similar to licensure in some ways, although it differs in some significant aspects. Certification and licensure both are voluntary and have established qualification requirements regarding training and experience, Also, both rely on some measure of knowledge and/or competence to determine which applicants have met the standards. Both charge fees and require continuing education for professional renewal. Licensure, however, is a statutory process by which an agency of government, usually a state, grants permission to a person meeting predetermined standards to engage in a given occupation or use a particular title and perform specified functions (Fretz & Mills, 1980; Baruth & Huber, 1985). Licensure is also geographically restricted to the state in which it is issued.

Certification is a nonstatutory process by which a governmental body, agency, or association grants recognition to an individual for having met certain predetermined professional qualifications. Licensure gives the practitioner the legal right to practice through statute, whereas certification gives standardized recognition of competence by a professional group or governmental unit. Licensure authorizes the holder to practice, whereas certification does not grant such authority.

Counselors who meet specified standards can attain certification in a number of areas and through a variety of methods. Both the various areas and methods will be presented in this chapter. A counselor may, for example, attain generic counselor certification through the National Board for Certified Counselors. A counselor may obtain the generic NBCC certification and then qualify for specialty certification through the NBCC. Counselors seeking and meeting other specialty standards can be certified independently from the NBCC process through the National Academy of Certified Clinical Mental Health Counselors or the Commission on Rehabilitation Counselor Certification. It is possible for counselors to be certified by other agencies not affiliated with the American Association of Counseling and Development, such as certification as a sex counselor by the American Association of Sex Educator Counselors and Therapists (AASECT) *or* as a marriage and family therapist by the American Association for Marriage and Family Therapy.

The benefits of certification are:

1. *Professional identity*. Certification as a National Certified Counselor (NCC) identifies the individual as a professionally certified counselor and a distinctive professional within the mental health field; certification as a Certified Clinical Mental Health Counselor (CCMHC), Certified Rehabilitation Counselor (CRC), or National Certified Career Counselor (NCCC) indicates that the individual is a specialist within the counseling profession.
2. *Visibility*. Certified counselors are listed in registers that are made available to mental health centers and to consumer, insurance, and medical organizations.
3. *Credibility*. Certification procedures are consistent with established national guidelines and backed by an organization with a code of ethics and procedures for handling consumer ethical complaints.
4. *Flexibility*. Certification is considered to be of value to counselors who can transfer their certification from one state to another.
5. *Continued professional growth*. Because of continuing education requirements for recertification, the skills of certified counselors can remain current and the consumer is better served (Peterson & Nisenholz, 1987; Messina, 1979, 1985; Stone, 1985).

Registry

Registry is closely related to certification. Counselor certifying groups such as NBCC, NACCMHC, and CRCC publish registries or lists of professional counselors who have qualified for the credential. Vac and Loesch (1987) maintain the distinguishing feature between registry and certification is intent. In certification, the primary intent is to become certified with the listing in the agency registry as a byproduct. With registry, the intent is to be placed on the list, such as the roster of the Council for the National Register of Health Service Providers in Psychology. Both processes have the goal of identifying individuals who have met a set of professional standards and then providing the public with the names of these qualified professionals.

Registries are also a product of certification processes. NBCC, NACCMHC, and CRCC each publish a registry of those professional counselors they have certified. Registries are important for the public relations function they serve for counselors and the profession (Loesch & Vac, 1985).

National Generic Certification for Counselors

The National Board for Certified Counselors is the independent, non-profit, voluntary certifying organization whose primary purpose is to identify to professionals and the general public those counselors who have voluntarily sought and obtained certification, and to maintain a register of those counselors. Counselors certified by NBCC are authorized to use the designation "NCC," which stands for National Certified Counselor. These counselors meet the professional standards established by the board and abide by the NBCC code of ethics, which is identical to the AACD code. To be certified, a counselor must have a master's or doctoral degree in counseling or a closely related field from a regionally accredited university, have at least 2 years professional counseling experience, have documented supervised counseling experience, provide three character references, and take a standardized written examination. Certification is for a period of 5 years with 100 hours of accrued continuing education credit required during that period. Nearly 17,300 counselors have been certified by NBCC since the process began (T.W. Clawson, personal communication, April 18, 1990).

Specialty Certification Combined With Generic NCC Certification

National Certified Career Counselor

Beginning in 1985, NBCC assumed responsibility for administering the certification program previously supported by the National Career Development Association for career counselors. By completing the requirements for this certification, including an examination and additional academic, experiential, and reference requirements, a counselor who has been previously certified as a NCC counselor can secure speciality certification as a National Certified Career Counselor (Vac & Loesch, 1987).

New Specialities

NBCC has now established standards and is developing the procedures for additional speciality certification for those interested in gerontological counseling and school counseling. These national speciality certifications will be available before the end of 1992 (T.W. Clawson, personal communication, April 18, 1990). The certification titles will be something like National Certified School Counselor (NCSC) and National Certified Gerontological Counselor (NCGC). The recent formation of the International Association of Marriage and Family Counselors (IAMFC) as a division in AACD is likely to result in another certification speciality area.

It is important to understand that the NBCC certification process is considered to be a generic certification appropriate for all counselors, and that those who attain this certification have demonstrated minimum competence levels generally considered to be important for all counselors. It is assumed that all counselors must know some of the same things and be able to do some of the same things (Vac & Loesch, 1987). The specialty certification processes, then, are an effort to recognize those professionals who have both the generic competence and the speciality preparation and experience that shows them to have gone beyond the basic competencies and have acquired the necessary training and experience to work effectively in a specialization area.

Speciality Certification Without Generic Certification

Mental Health Counselors

The American Mental Health Counselors Association was founded in 1976 and established an independent certification system for mental health counselors in 1978. This is a speciality certification program that is not built on the generic base of NBCC certification as described above. The effort of the AMHCA group was to forgo the generic NBCC certification requirements and certify for one specialization only—mental health counselors. Applicants must have a master's degree in mental health counseling or an allied mental health field and 2 years of postmaster's work experience, which includes 3,000 hours of clinical work and 100 hours of face-to-face supervision; provide a video sample of counseling skills; and complete a 4-hour multiple-choice examination covering mental health counseling. The examination is waived for persons who are licensed professional counselors in a state having counselor licensure. One hundred hours of continuing education credit is required every 5 years to maintain the credential. The certification status awarded is Certified Clinical Mental Health Counselor. The certifying body is the National Academy of Certified Clinical Mental Health Counselors. There are currently 12,000 members of AMHCA: 1,200 are certificants, and 700 are CCMHCs (Herman, 1990).

Rehabilitation Counselors

A second speciality certification area that offers certification independently from NBCC certification is that provided by the Commission on Rehabilitation Counselor Certification. CRCC was formed in 1973 as a result of cooperative work between the members of the National Rehabilitation Counseling Association (NRCA) and the American Rehabilitation Counseling Association (ARCA). The first rehabilitation counselors were certified in 1974, and there are now over 11,000 certified individuals. The designation for this credential is Certified Rehabilitation Counselor (CRC) (Hedgeman, 1985). A CRC can become a NCC by paying the required fees and verifying CRC certification. There are seven differing options an applicant can follow to obtain CRC certification. These include completion of a graduate degree in rehabilitation counseling, passing a 300-item multiple-choice examination, completion of a 600-hour internship, and completion of some variable amount of work experience depending on the option selected. Every 5 years 150 clock hours of renewal credit are required to qualify for recertification.

Other Speciality Certifications for Counselors

There are a number of other independently operated certification bodies that provide credentials which may be of interest to counselors. The American Association for Marriage and Family Therapy provides a credential similar to a certificate for those who meet the standards. AAMFT is not a division of AACD and is not affiliated with NBCC.

The International Association of Marriage and Family Counselors was approved as a division within AACD in 1989 and will be developing some form of credentialing in the near future for counselors who are interested in marriage and family counseling but wish to maintain affiliation and credentialing with the counseling body.

There are also other speciality professional certifying bodies which are of interest to counselors but not under the AACD umbrella. The names and addresses of these groups are provided in appendix B.

Overview of the Chronology of Counselor Certification

School Counselor Certification 1940–1960

Although the literature does not clearly show the beginnings of certification processes for school counselors, it is known that the process began
during the 1940s or 1950s with state departments of education certifying
school counselors. It is also known that the process was inextricably en-
meshed in the process of public school teacher certification.

Borow (1964) reported a study by Jones and Miller showing that, in
1954, 39 states provided some guidance services in the schools, and that
although certification was mandatory in 21 states, less than half of these
counselors had any courses in counseling. Borow further stated that 43%
of the schools in Ohio had secondary school counselor during 1959 but that
only 32% of full-time counselors were certified.

Dugan (1962) reported on the status of school counselor certification
from 1960 data and indicated that, although 38 states at that time reported
certification requirements for school counselors, the quality of these requirements was extremely low. His data showed that 39 of the 50 states
only required from one-half a master's degree (15 hours) down to no professional graduate work. He decried the lack of professionalism such data
indicated.

In 1965, Keppers proposed that the time had arrived to achieve the
goals of program accreditation and national certification for counselors.
Pietrofesa and Vriend (1971) reported that Michigan was the last state to
establish some state certification for school counselors when the counselor
certification law went into effect in that state in 1971. Wellner (1983), reporting on the status of state school counselor certification in more recent
times, indicated that, even in 1983, only 23 states required a master's degree
in guidance and counseling in order to be certified as a school counselor.

Rehabilitation Counselor Certification 1960–1974

Rehabilitation counseling certification originated in the late 1960s when
rehabilitation counselors belonging to two different organizations began to
work together toward this end. Rehabilitation counselors from the National
Rehabilitation Counselors Association and those with the AACD division,
the American Rehabilitation Counselors Association, developed a certification process in 1973. The first counselors were certified in 1974, and this
body has been certifying rehabilitation counselors since that time independently of NBCC.

Mental Health Counselor Certification 1976–1979

The American Mental Health Counselors Association was founded in November 1976 and currently has about 12,000 members. The first mental health counselors were certified in 1979, and AMHCA continues to certify this one specialization independent of NBCC.

National Board for Certified Counselors Established 1979–1983

Definitive steps were taken in 1979 to establish what would become known as NBCC. Lloyd A. Stone chaired the AACD committee from 1979 to 1982 and served as the chair of the NBCC Board from 1982 to 1985. The first counselors to be nationally certified were recognized in 1983. Since that time, 17,300 counselors have achieved this certification.

National Certified Career Counselor 1981–1985

The movement toward certification for career counselors was begun in 1981, and in 1984 the first 300 career counselors were certified. In 1985 the certification process was given over to NBCC by the National Council for Credentialing Career Counselors (NCCCC). There are currently about 925 certified career counselors.

Projections for the Future

Based upon the current numbers of voluntary certifying bodies for counselors, it appears that the counseling profession may be suffering from "over-kill" in the area of certification. However, as stated earlier, NBCC is in the process of establishing standards for certifying gerontological counselors and school counselors. Other specialities that are frequently discussed are certification for employment counselors, marriage and family counselors, counselor supervisors, and multicultural counselors. It would be impossible to predict how many counselor specialty certification standards might be established by the turn of the century. If additional certifications are to be appropriately implemented, and have a chance for survival, it is apparent that new standards should be based upon established needs and then developed and coordinated under the National Board for Certified Counselors umbrella. Thomas W. Clawson (1990b), executive director of NBCC, announced in a letter to counselor education students that Maryland and Washington State Boards of Education now accept the NCC designation as having fulfilled the requirements for certification as a school counselor. This is, to say the least, an encouragement for the further development of school counselor certification standards by NBCC. Perhaps the day will come when all states require school counselor certification through NBCC.

The future for counselor certification appears bright for at least the next decade or two. In the final analysis, the primary purpose of all counselor credentialing is to improve the quality of services to clients. It would appear that counselor certification is rapidly moving toward this end.

References

Baruth, L.G., & Huber, C.H. (1985). *Counseling and psychotherapy: Theoretical analysis and skills applications.* Columbus, OH: Charles E. Merrill.

Baruth, L.G., & Robinson, E.H. (1987). *An introduction to the counseling profession.* Englewood Cliffs, NJ: Prentice Hall. In Borow, H. (1964). *Man in a world at work.* Boston: Houghton Mifflin.

Clawson, T.W. (1990, April). Letter to recent graduates with master's degrees in counseling. Alexandria, VA: National Board for Certified Counselors.

Dugan, W.E. (1962). An inward look at assumption and aspirations. *Counselor Education and Supervision, 1*(4), 174–180.

Forster, J.R. (1977). What shall we do about credentialing? *Personnel and Guidance Journal, 55*(8), 573–576.

Fretz, B.R., & Mills, D.H. (1980). *Licensing and certification of psychologists and counselors: A guide to current policies, procedures, and legislation.* San Francisco: Jossey-Bass.

Hedgeman, B.S. (1985). Rehabilitation counselor certification. *Journal of Counseling and Development, 63*(6), 609–610.

Herman, J.H. (1990, January). President elect's column. *The Advocate,* p.2.

Keppers, G.L. (1965). National certification of counselors. *Counselor Education and Supervision, 4,* 203–207.

Loesch, L.C. (1984). Professional credentialing in counseling. *Counseling and Human Development, 17*(2), 1–11.

Loesch, L.C., & Vac, N.D. (1985). *National counselor certification examination preliminary technical manual.* Alexandria, VA: National Board for Certified Counselors/American Association for Counseling and Development.

Messina, J. (1979). The National Academy of Certified Clinical Mental Health Counselors: Creating a new professional identity. *AMHCA Journal, 1*(6), 607–608.

Messina, J. (1985). The National Academy of Certified Mental Health Counselors: Creating a new professional identity. *Journal of Counseling and Development, 63*(10), 607–608.

Peterson, J.V., & Nisenholz, B. (1987). *Orientation to counseling.* Boston: Allyn & Bacon.

Pietrofesa, J., & Vriend, J. (1971). *The school counselor as a professional.* Itaska, IL: E.E. Peacock.

Stone, L. (1985). National Board for Certified Counselors: History, relationships, and projections. *Journal of Counseling and Development, 63*(10), 605–606.

Vac, N.A., & Loesch, L.C. (1987). *Counseling as a profession.* Muncie, IN: Accelerated Development.

Wellner, J. (1983). *Teachers, counselors, librarians, administrators: Requirements for certification.* Chicago: University of Chicago Press.

CHAPTER 3

Historical Antecedents and Current Status of Counselor Licensure

Thomas W. Hosie

Occupational licensure is viewed as one of the most important characteristics that define an occupation as a profession. Through the statute that provides for licensing, a profession attains almost total self-regulation. Attaining licensure also increases the status of a profession and brings other benefits because the practice of the profession is deemed significant for the health and welfare of the public and therefore must be regulated to protect the public from untrained or incompetent practitioners. Licensure is one type of credentialing. However, it is thought to be the most important and the culminating type for a profession. Historically, the other types of credentialing have provided the bases for licensure.

Since the middle 1970s the American Association for Counseling and Development and its divisional associations have aggressively pursued licensure for counselors. The counselor licensure movement has been highly successful. Statutory regulations governing counselors have been passed in 34 states. The rate of passage of counselor licensure acts, given the same time frame, has been greater than the passage of similar state legislation for any of the other social science professions. The need to regulate a profession and enact licensing legislation is often cited to be the protection of the public from untrained and incompetent practitioners. However, the history of licensing of the professions, including the social science professions, indicates that there are many motives for the pursuit of licensing. The counselor licensure movement is no different, and probably counselors would not have made such giant strides without the motivation produced by the licensing activities of psychologists. Much of the information in this chapter focuses on the history of licensing and the licensing activities of psychologists. Professions appear to go through similar evolutionary processes in striving for licensure, and counselors can learn from the activities of psychologists and other professions. Perhaps even more important is the understanding that counselors can gain from looking at the competition and territorial disputes among the social science professions.

The motives to pursue licensing and the ability of licensure statutes to ensure competent practice for the public form complex issues. Although counselors have learned much in the past 15 years about licensure, the basic issues involved in licensing still remain and must be understood and dealt with by counselors if we are to be successful in the states without counselor licensure and also in working with the other social science professions.

Note that state statutes are constantly being revised, and licensure boards have the capacity to write additional rules and regulations. Thus, some of the information in this chapter may not be up to date when it appears in print.

Early History of Professional Regulation and Licensing

The beginning of the regulation of professions can be traced to Frederick II, 13th-century emperor of the Holy Roman Empire, who enacted the first medical practice act. The requirements he set forth for the practice of medicine included (a) passing an examination by a teacher of medicine, (b) completing 3 years of the study of logic, and (c) 1 year of practice under an experienced physician after 5 years of study. Other provisions of the act included (a) punishments for offenses, (b) the setting of fees, and (c) prohibitions on a physician owning an apothecary shop (Gross, 1978). The major effect of implementing those training requirements for physicians was that everyone except university-trained physicians was prohibited from practicing medicine (Ehrenreich & English, 1973). In addition to setting the standard of limiting practice of a profession to university-trained individuals, many provisions of the act have been maintained and are included in current acts governing the professions.

The requirement of university training as the minimum standard for practice in the professions during the Middle Ages was created by associations or guilds of teachers and students. The degrees issued by the universities were considered certificates of competency for professional practice and usually entitled the graduate to exclusive rights to practice. In effect, the universities trained and then licensed individuals. The guilds, which later evolved into professional societies, acted in a similar manner by trying to give exclusive rights of practice to their members (Gerstle & Jacobs, 1976). During the decline of the guilds in Europe, states increased their authority over training and licensing requirements. At least in the beginning, states were motivated by a common purpose, namely to insure fair dealing, protect the public against quackery and incompetence, and lift the standards of the professions by means of better professional training and testing of professional competence. However, the states continually relied on universities and other institutions to train practitioners for the professions (Carman, 1958). Although the effectiveness of licensing regulations by states was limited because of the need to serve the masses beyond that which licensed practitioners could provide, Gross (1978) points out that the intermingling of state and university or association regulations was an attempt to use the authority of the state to legitimize an occupation (Fretz & Mills, 1980).

Licensing in the United States

The evolution of the regulation of the professions in the United States is characterized by movement from one extreme to another. During the Colonial Period, European immigrants came to this country with a variety of economic, political, and religious beliefs. Many fled from an oppressive existence and brought little with them. The various licensing systems in Europe at the time seemed to exert little influence on the colonists. There were few universities in America during the Colonial Period, and most were dedicated to training individuals for the ministry. Although the major professions of the time, such as law, medicine, the ministry, and teaching, were represented in Colonial America, those who could afford the cost of a university education for one of the professions went to Europe for training. Because most individuals could not go to Europe, and because the demand for services far outdistanced that which university graduates could supply, most individuals apprenticed under a degreed practitioner. This preparation for the professions almost solely limited to the apprentice system brought about attempts to raise training and practice standards in post-Revolutionary America (Carman, 1958). Shortly before 1800 many states gave almost absolute power to medical societies to regulate the examination and licensing of medical practitioners (Spector & Frederick, 1952). Such control by the state and professional associations paralleled the development of medical schools in this country. However, a two-tiered system of university training and apprenticeship was maintained (Shryock, 1967), and this system continued for many professions well into the 20th century.

Many of the modern day professional associations were organized prior to the Civil War. The American Medical Association was the first to organize in 1847, and the American Pharmaceutical Association, American Dental Association, and American Veterinary Medical Association followed (Angel, 1970). Beginning in the late 1830s states began to repeal and withdraw many of the restrictions for professional licensing and practice. At the outbreak of the Civil War no state had an effective system for licensing professionals (Carman, 1958; Spector & Frederick, 1952). Carman (1958) lists the following as reasons why states abandoned regulation of the professions: (a) a growing spirit of democracy and individualism, (b) government support of greater economic freedom and a laissez-faire philosophy to enhance development, (c) a growing and expanding population demanding more professional practitioners, (d) bickering among groups within a profession, and (e) a decentralized administration as the machinery to implement the rules and regulations for practice in rural areas. Additional reasons, voiced as complaints to legislatures from the populace, were that the professions (a) constituted monopolies and restrained trade, (b) maintained a class system that blocked the entrance of lower classes, and (c) discouraged and blocked development in nonorthodox areas of practice (Tabachnik, 1976). The needs of an expanding nation took precedence over rigorous controls limiting the number of practitioners and the services they offered.

Soon after the Civil War the trend of deregulation was reversed. Many college and universities were established during the decades following the Civil War, and opportunity for education and entrance into the professions increased. Many professional associations were established, and the existing associations increased their memberships and became stronger. The American Medical Association, after establishing itself as the preeminent medical association, was able to exclude all groups that did not conform to its standards of training and practice (Belcher, 1973). The pre-Civil-War deregulation of the professions and relaxed training standards had opened the door for inadequate professional practitioners. The public became disillusioned and supported more stringent regulations on professional training and practice. The professional associations and societies seized the opportunity and, during the last two decades of the 19th century, lobbied legislatures for more regulation. At this time the legal and medical professions cited the connection between competence and regulation that forms the rationale for our current licensing practices (Tabachnik, 1976).

The licensure movement in the 20th century has expanded to include many professions. Apprentice programs have almost totally been replaced by university training programs. University training has been lengthened, and internships occur after training is completed. Also, the type of regulation sought on behalf of professions has moved from certification of title to licensing the practice of the profession (Gross, 1978).

The Roles of Professional Associations

The purpose of professional associations is to provide a means for members to come together to share knowledge and attempt to solve common problems. Association members meet at state, regional, and national gatherings to discuss their experiences, gain feedback, and develop new techniques and methods. These meetings, together with the published accounts of findings, ultimately expand the knowledge base of the profession. The shared knowledge base and goals produce a professional identity that is maintained and enhanced by association activities.

The professional associations that were established during the middle and late 1800s had other common goals beyond the of advancement of knowledge within their professions. These associations produced the standards of occupational behavior to give their constituents widespread public acceptance as members of unique and high-standing professions. The attainment of professional status is embodied in the licensure legislation the associations were able to acquire. During the early period of their existence these associations raised the standards for entrance into the professions and established codes of conduct and penalties for misconduct. Association recommendations on governance of their professions were adopted by state legislatures, which in effect gave the recommendations legal standing and also gave the associations control over the professions. The legislation determined who could enter and practice the professions, which had the effect of bestowing a distinct and high level of status on anyone obtaining the license. The associations maintained control of their professions by having provisions within the law that guaranteed them representation on the state boards that regulated entrance into and practice of the professions.

Characteristics of a Profession

Sociologists have studied the growth of professions and specified the characteristics or traits that exemplify an occupation attaining professional status (Barber, 1965; Elliott, 1972; Goode, 1960; Pavalko, 1971). The enactment of licensing legislation is viewed as the single most important ingredient in enabling an occupation to reach professional status. Among characteristics often cited as determining professional status are (a) that the profession determines its own training and education standards and controls the practices of services, (b) that the profession determines the members of the state regulatory board, (c) that the profession has broad authority over the rules and regulations governing the profession, and (d) that the profession stipulates a code of practice or ethics with regulatory control of licensee behavior. Another characteristic of a profession is that the practitioner is relatively free from outside or public control (Goode, 1960). All of these characteristics are embedded in the state regulatory acts licensing a profession.

But there are other traits commonly used to distinguish an occupation as a profession that are not embedded within licensing statutes. The regulations in licensing statutes have, however, the effect of helping to produce the outcomes that have been characterized as traits of professional standing. Among these characteristics also denoting a profession are (a) that the profession is primarily interested in community service rather than self-interest, (b) that the members of the profession strongly identify with and are highly committed to that profession, and (c) that the profession is viewed as a terminal occupation and a life-long commitment. These characteristics are produced by the evolution of a profession through the establishment and activities of a professional society that culminate in the attainment of licensure.

Criticisms of Licensure Regulations

There have been many criticisms of the motivations of professional societies to pursue licensure. Many of those criticisms have come from psychologists (e.g., Bernstein & Lecomte, 1981; Danish & Smyer, 1981; Gross, 1978; Meltzer, 1975). Five beliefs promulgated by professional societies in support of licensing that have received extensive criticism are discussed by Fretz and Mills (1980). Among these beliefs are (a) that licensing protects the public by setting minimum standards for service providers, (b) that licensing protects the public from its own ignorance, (c) that licensure makes practitioners more competent and better distributed, (d) that licensure upgrades the profession, and (e) that licensure helps to define the profession. The licensing of a profession produces positive effects in each of the areas mentioned. However, the criticisms focus on the negative, restrictive effects that licensing laws produce and the lack of alternative systems within licensing legislation to meet the needs of the public.

Licensing regulations and restrictions have had a paramount effect on the evolution of the social science professions and have been powerful motivators in determining the goals and activities of the associations in the mental health field. The number of psychologists rapidly increased after World War II, and one of the major institutional employers of psychologists was the Veterans Administration. Psychologists practiced in that setting under the supervision of psychiatrists and saw themselves highly restricted in their practice because of existing medical licensing statutes and the traditional dominance of MDs in a hospital setting (Cummings, 1990). The restrictions placed on psychologists motivated them to form stronger association alliances and begin the process of a national movement to secure state licensing. The rapid increase in the number of psychological licensing laws and attempts to restrict practice in the mental health field to psychologists provided powerful motivation for social workers and mental health counselors to seek licensing.

The positive effects of licensing emphasized to legislators and the public by psychologists (Fretz & Mills, 1980) and the criticisms of those effects also played a significant role in motivating mental health counselors to organize and seek licensing. Acknowledging the types of criticisms of licensing legislation seems to have produced a desirable effect on the types of provisions written into counselor licensing acts. Thus, the goals of licensing legislation and the criticisms of the processes to reach those goals are worthy of some discussion.

That licensing of psychologists and other professionals protects the public by setting minimum educational standards for practice and that licensure makes practitioners more competent are positions that have been severely and similarly criticized. The criticisms focus on the incongruence between training and practice and on the means of establishing and maintaining competency. Entrance into a social science profession by attaining a university degree and passing a pencil-and-paper examination does not provide assurance of competent practice and protection of the public. University training is highly academic and usually does not emphasize the practice of a profession. This emphasis on academics over practice in psychology led to the growth of professional psychology and the establishment of professional schools of psychology (Cummings, 1990).

Much of the training for practice of psychology is left to the 1-year internship following attainment of a degree. Although internships can be highly structured and of substantial benefit, they last only 1 year and come at the beginning of the professional's career. The succeeding 1 or 2 years of supervision under state board control usually lack specific rules and can simply be a monitoring process. Supervisors usually have no formal training and rely on their own apprenticeship experiences. In the social sciences are many areas of study and practitioner settings. Because the license is a certificate for generic practice, there may be only general rules for matching the knowledge and experience areas of the supervisor and supervisee.

Licensure board examinations are constructed to reflect knowledge of practice, but they do not directly measure how a person behaves in his or her interaction with clients. Also, licensing examinations are generic measures and do not specifically cover all the areas in which individuals specialize. In the social science field there are many different theories of human behavior, and the licensing examinations are unable to measure the practitioner's efficiency in interacting with clients based on those theories. Ensuring competence of practitioners can only be accomplished by monitoring their behavior at different times in their careers. Although there have been initial attempts by professions in that area, there are no licensing acts that mandate such procedures.

A major difficulty that plagues the social science professions in establishing "standards of practice" is that there are many different methods and techniques based on many theories of human behavior that do not have sufficient research support to determine what is and what isn't effective practice. Hence, regulation of the profession is accomplished by enforcing codes of ethics rather that specific standards of practice. Attempts to rectify the problems associated with minimum standards have consisted of increasing those standards. However, increasing standards has had the undesirable effect of producing additional restrictions on entering the profession and restricting the practice of other professionals.

Two other seemingly positive effects of licensing—upgrading the profession and further definition of the profession—are severely criticized because the activities to produce both these outcomes have had the effect of limiting practice in the social sciences to one or two professions. Upgrading the professions has thus far relied on increasing and further specifying university training requirements and enlarging the scope of training, which increases the potential areas for practice. Creating more specific guidelines for training restricts all but those who meet the requirements from practicing the profession. Alternative routes of study or curricula are not honored. As the knowledge base of a profession enlarges and more specialty areas are devised, the definition of practice of the profession encompasses more of human behavior. The history of attempts at defining a social science profession shows that those attempts do not produce more specificity for practice. Rather, more extensive definitions are created that evolve into attempts to restrict mental health practices to that profession.

All the provisions of any licensing act aim to produce a system that has the effect of protecting the public. Although there are benefits for the public, there are also indications that the costs of services rise and people in rural areas and the poor receive fewer services. Undeniably, however, licensing has greatly enhanced the professions that have attained that type of regulatory power.

Types of Credentialing

The most often used means within the social science professions to protect the public are licensure and certification of practitioners. Licensure is a statutory process whereby a governmental agency grants permission to an individual who has been found to meet minimal competency standards to engage in the practice of an occupation. Meeting minimal standards to undertake the practice of the occupation is viewed as a requirement to insure the public health, safety, and welfare against unauthorized, untrained, and inadequately trained individuals in the practice of that occupation. Licensure statutes are often called *practice acts* because they determine, from the definition of the practice of the occupation in the statute, what a licensed person can do and what others cannot do. Occupational titles indicate the practice of a profession to the public, and for public welfare, the use of specific occupational titles is restricted by the licensure statute.

In comparison, certification is a process whereby a government agency or association grants recognition to an individual who has met certain minimal qualifications specified by the certifying agency. Certification procedures can be statutory or nonstatutory, depending on the type of agency that grants the certification. Certification statutes are often called *title acts* because they determine, by the qualifications set forth, who can use a particular designation or title. Use of the "certified" title informs the public of individuals who have met the qualifications to be certified.

Licensing acts are intended to govern the practice of a profession to insure the quality of practice, whereas certification is a notification that an individual has met certain standards for practice of a profession. Certification, like licensure, can restrict the practice of a profession. For example, in most educational districts individuals seeking to be school counselors or school psychologists must be certified by the state, and noncertified people cannot hold those positions. In the mental health professions, the effects of so-called *licensure acts* can be confusing because many of the acts have no clauses to regulate the behavior of the licensee or to restrict the practice of the profession. Although these acts grant licenses, they amount to certification legislation. Historically, most of the professions began with the passing of certification acts and only later were those acts changed to true licensure legislation.

Another means of notification to the public and agencies of individual qualifications is registration or listing. Registries set forth minimal qualifications and list the names of individuals who meet those qualifications. Often the registry uses standards of other groups and requires that individuals be certified or licensed by those groups to be listed in the registry. Registration is voluntary and is simply a means of providing information about those who have certain qualifications to provide a particular service. Physician and nurse registries are examples of local registries that provide the public and agencies with lists of qualified individuals who can be contacted for services.

Licensing of Psychologists and Insurance Reimbursement

Professional psychology blazed the trail for the nonmedical professions to obtain licensure and professional status by challenging psychiatry's dominance of the field in order to become an independent health provider (Cummings, 1990; Danish & Smyer, 1981). The need to establish parity with psychiatry and not remain under its jurisdiction when providing treatment was a dominant motivational theme in psychologists' pursuit of licensure. Mack (1982) gives an account of the enactment of legislation governing psychological practice (which is used as a source for much of the information provided in this section). The first psychological licensing act was passed in the state of Connecticut in 1945. During the next 10 years only six states enacted legislation governing the psychological profession. From 1956 to 1965 state legislatures in 16 states passed some form of regulation for the practice of psychology. Thus, by 1965 one-half of the 50 states had some form of legislation regulating the practice of psychology. The period 1966 to 1975 saw the greatest increase in psychological licensing laws, with an additional 22 states granting psychologists some form of regulation over their profession. By 1978, all 50 states, the District of Columbia, and seven Canadian provinces had passed legislation concerning certification, registration, or licensing of psychologists (Fretz & Mills, 1980).

Social work followed the lead of the psychological profession, attaining licensure legislation about one decade later (Cummings, 1990). A brief history of social work adds to our understanding of the current status of licensure in the social science professions: The first regulatory legislation for social work was passed in Puerto Rico in 1934, and California enacted regulations in 1945. No other states or territories enacted any social work regulation until 1961. From 1961 to 1970, 7 states enacted some form of regulation, and by 1977, 23 states had regulations governing social work practices (Mack, 1982). Forty-eight states, the District of Columbia, Puerto Rico, and the Virgin Islands currently have some form of legislation regulating social work (Garcia, 1990).

Much of the motivation for psychological licensing in the late 1960s and 1970s comes from the pursuit of third-party payments and inclusion in national health insurance by psychologists (Cummings, 1990; Gross, 1978; Meltzer, 1975). A number of events prompted psychologists to move in that direction. Because of the increased growth of new licensing legislation in the health fields, the U.S. Department of Health, Education, and Welfare (HEW) was ordered by the 91st Congress under Public Law 91-519 to prepare a report identifying the major problems associated with licensure, certification, and other qualifications for the employment and practice of health personnel to maximize services to the population. Although the HEW *Report on Licensure and Related Health Personnel Credentialing* (1971) presented to the Congress emphasized the regulations of the physical health professions, the study included the regulatory practices of psychology and social work. Counseling was not listed as an occupation in the report. HEW reported that the state laws regulating the health and mental health professions were conflicting, restrictive, and inconsistent from state to state (Mack, 1982). No federal requirements were in effect at that time to regulate any of the nonmedical occupations listed in the report (Mack, 1982). The report recommended that states adopt national examinations emphasizing proficiency standards for entrance into the profession and that state boards create requirements ensuring a continued level of competence for maintaining a license. In a follow-up HEW report by Cohen and Miike (1973), the authors concluded from their investigation that nonuniform state licensing codes were a direct obstacle to the geographic mobility of health personnel and posed a serious problem for adequate distribution of services in the United States. They also concluded that some licensing laws regulating mental health, although purported to be in the public interest, prevented qualified practitioners from serving needed segments of the population. The APA Committee on State Legislation, founded in the 1950s, and the

American Association of State Psychology Boards (AASPB), founded in 1961, both worked on the task of standardizing state licensing regulations. Specifically, the AASPB was founded because of differences in state licensure laws and moves by psychologists (Fretz & Mills, 1980). Both groups attempted to resolve major issues facing the profession, one of which was attaching reimbursement from medical insurers to licensing status.

The need to provide a means of identifying individuals who could provide psychological services prompted the American Psychological Association to establish in 1975 the National Register for Health Service Providers in Psychology, a national register of qualified providers. Creating this method of identification was a direct attempt to counter insurance companies' criticisms that they could not identify qualified practitioners for payment and to include psychologists in federal legislation on reimbursement (Meltzer, 1975). The Register was also the first attempt by psychology to attain national recognition and lay the ground work for continued advancement for inclusion in federal programs.

Cummings (1990) describes the events of the late 1950s that led to the APA fight to achieve national recognition and third-party reimbursement. He cites the warnings of Leonard Small, a New York psychologist, as beginning the advocacy movement within APA for third-party recognition. Small "argued that if psychology were not recognized as a primary mental health provider by insurance carriers and the government, who would make up the third-party payers, the profession of psychology would suffer economic extinction" (p. 486). Cummings recounts that Small and a group of activists were able to convince the APA to look into the reimbursement issue and that APA formed the Ad Hoc Committee on Insurance and Related Social Developments in 1963. Five years later APA formed a standing Committee on Health Insurance that devised the concept of "freedom-of-choice legislation." In using that concept, state insurance codes were amended so that any health insurance company that reimburses for the services of a psychiatrist must also reimburse for the services of a qualified psychologist. All but eight states have such freedom-of-choice legislation today (Cummings, 1990).

The possibility of national health insurance (NHI) and the benefits to be derived by psychologists maintained the drive for third-party reimbursement. Thus, having established licensing for psychologists in all 50 states, the focus shifted to incorporation of reimbursement requirements within federal legislation (Mack, 1982). This drive for inclusion in federal programs and national recognition enabled psychologists to obtain legal recognition and direct access for services and payments within the federal Civilian Health and Medical Program of the Uniformed Services for dependents of military personnel and the Civilian Health and Medical Program of the Veterans Administration for dependents of totally disabled veterans. Also, through effective lobbying, psychologists were included in the Rehabilitation Act of 1973 to provide independent services and in the 1974 Federal Employees' Benefit Act, which covers

federal workers. In addition, psychologists were included in the Health Maintenance Organization Act of 1973 to deliver independent services for reimbursement (Kiesler & Zaro, 1981). In 1989 psychologists finally obtained provider
status within Medicare (Cummings, 1990), the last federal program in which
they had not been included.

The Restrictive Effects of State Licensure of Psychologists

The APA Committee on Legislation established in the early 1950s
published a set of guidelines in 1955 for licensing of psychologists. The
committee's function was "to call to the attention of states seeking legislation
projected provisions in state laws which might set unfortunate precedents
for psychology as a whole, or unduly restrict or subordinate the professional
activities of psychologists, or other legitimate professions" (APA, 1967,
p. 1097). The committee also served as a consultant to states to handle their
problems with state legislatures and at the same time adhere to APA policies.
The committee recommended that state legislation take the form of certification, although the development of licensing legislation was encouraged.
A specific definition for psychological practice was not given. Three levels
of practice were recommended with preference given to a one-level law
requiring the doctoral degree. There were 36 states with legislation regulating psychology. Some form of the word *license* was used in many of
those statutes, but the statutes were certification acts and did not infringe
on the practices of counselors.

In 1967, the APA Committee on Legislation published a new set of APA-
approved recommendations with a model for state legislation that sent shock
waves through the counseling profession. The new recommended changes in
psychological regulations—and the number of states already possessing psychology statutes—frightened counselors. Specifically, the committee recommended that states seek licensing laws regulating the practice of psychology.
The committee defined the practice of psychology:

> as rendering to individuals, groups, organizations, institutions, or to
> the public any psychological service involving the application of prin-
> ciples, methods, and procedures of understanding, predicting, and in-
> fluencing behavior, such as principles pertaining to learning, perception,
> motivation, thinking, emotions, mind-body relationships, and inter-
> personal relationships; of the methods and procedures of interviewing,
> consulting, counseling, and psychotherapy; of constructing, adminis-
> tering, and interpreting of tests of mental abilities, aptitudes, interests,
> attitudes, personality characteristics, emotions, and motivation; and of
> addressing public opinion.
>
> The application of said principles and methods includes but is not
> restricted to diagnosis, prevention, and amelioration of adjustment prob-

lems and emotional and mental disorders of individuals and groups; hypnosis; educational and vocational counseling; personnel selection and management; the evaluation and planning of effective work and learning situations; advertising and market research; and the resolution of interpersonal and social conflicts.

Psychotherapy within the meaning of this act means the use of learning, conditioning methods, and emotional reactions, in a professional relationship, to assist a person or persons to modify feelings, attitudes, and behavior which are intellectually, socially, or emotionally maladjustive or ineffectual. (APA, 1967, p. 1099)

In addition, the committee recommended that "the practice of psychology should be restricted to one level, requiring a doctoral degree from an accredited college or university in a program that is primarily psychological and no less than 2 years of supervised experience, one of which is subsequent to the granting of the doctoral degree" (p. 1009). According to the provisions of the model legislation, although persons employed by accredited academic institutions, governmental agencies, research laboratories and business could provide services of a "psychological nature," they could not provide those services outside their agency or in private practice.

At the time of its reorganization in 1946, the American Psychological Association established the doctoral degree as the training standard for the profession. However, passing the recommended 1967 legislation would insure by law that only the those with a doctoral degree could practice psychology. That restriction would effectively stop master's-level individuals, at least in the private practice sector, from offering services defined as the practice of psychology. The definition of the practice of psychology presented by the APA Committee on Legislation was all encompassing of human behavior and even notes counseling as a method or procedure of practice. Granting psychologists sole auspices over the broad area of human behavior and the practices specified in the definition would disenfranchise counselors in private practice from their training and livelihood. Equally important was the wording of the exemption clauses and whether or not counselors working in public and nonprofit agencies would be affected. The model legislation was comprised of recommendations, and state psychological associations were free to disregard those recommendations when writing new legislation.

The effects of the APA licensing recommendations were felt in New York in the late 1960s and early 1970s. The state psychological association used a definition similar to that published in 1967 by the committee in the "Biondo licensing bill" in an attempt to revise the current statutes to restrict the practice of psychology. The intended effect of the legislation was to force public and nonprofit agencies to employ a psychologist to supervise the delivery of psychological services. Although that legislation was defeated three times and never passed, it signaled the potential effects of the new draft of legislative recommendations by APA. Sweeney and Sturdevant (1974) alerted counselors to the potential restrictive effects of the 1972 Ohio revised legislation licensing psychologists. They warned counselors that the broad definition of the practice of psychology in the law coupled with the wide discretionary powers of the board for enforcement might determine who could teach counseling courses outside departments of psychology. They also warned counselors of the potential restrictions of their practice of counseling within colleges and universities and other agencies.

The fears about the potential restrictions to be placed on the counseling profession by psychologists were well founded. The APA Legislative Committee in 1977 revised their recommendations for licensing of psychologists, proposing an even more restrictive model for legislation. The committee expanded the definition of psychology to include teaching and research. Although psychologists employed to carry out those functions were recommended to be exempt from licensing, no one else was. More importantly, the model legislation exemplified a "true" licensing bill. It covered people in all public and private institutions as well as in private practice. In addition, the recommendations specified that applicants for a license must possess a degree from a program of graduate study in psychology as defined by the board. Unless identified as an exempt profession, counselors would no longer be able to be trained or practice under such legislation. The recommendations of the committee were never adopted by APA. It is sufficient to say that such restrictions were even too restrictive for many psychologists.

Yet the committee's 1977 recommendations were incorporated within revised legislation proposed by many state psychological associations. State psychological associations in the 1980s in Florida and Louisiana were able to pass similar restrictions to those proposed by the committee in 1977 for training and the practice of psychology (counselors, through their own legislation in those states, were exempt from such restrictions). In 1987 the APA Council of Representatives passed a revision of the 1967 model for state legislation. The recommendations are not as restrictive as those of 1977. Most of the changes from 1967 have to do with psychologists themselves. However, a "true" licensing act is recommended, and only other recognized professions that are licensed, certified, or regulated under state laws and the clergy are exempted from regulation by the state board.

Licensing of Counselors

The determination of who is practicing psychology and the determination of who should be under the jurisdiction of a state board of psychologist examiners are extremely important for the counselor licensing movement. Understanding those questions and their answers provided counselors with the motivation and means to seek licensing for the profession. Specifically, in 1972 the Virginia State Board of Psychologist Examiners secured a court order to restrain John Weldon from conducting his private practice in career counseling. Weldon argued that guidance and counseling were separate fields from psychology and that he should not be under the jurisdiction of the board. The board disagreed saying that Weldon was practicing psychology. In October 1972 the court judge ruled ". . . the profession of personnel and guidance counseling is a separate profession (from psychology) and should be so recognized . . . However, this profession does utilize the tools of the psychologist . . . therefore it appears that there must be a regulatory body to govern the profession . . ." (Swanson, 1988, p. 1). Thus, because there was no regulatory body governing counseling in Virginia, Weldon was restrained from further practice. The judge "felt bound by the Virginia statute that 'appears to say' that if a counselor uses the tools of psychology, in the absence of a regulatory body governing guidance and counseling, a counselor in private practice is subject to the laws governing the practice of psychology" (Fretz & Mills, 1980, p. 80).

Armed with this court decision that made counselors in private practice like John Weldon unable to earn a livelihood, the Virginia Personnel and Guidance Association convinced legislators in 1975 to pass the first counselor regulatory act. That legislation established counseling as a profession separate from psychology in the state of Virginia. The legislation was revised in 1976 to provide licensing for counselors.

Prompted by several of its divisions, the American Association for Counseling and Development (at that time the American Personnel and Guidance Association) in 1974 adopted a position paper on "Licensing in the Helping Professions" in order to pursue "vigorous, responsible action to establish provisions for the licensure of professional counselors in the various states" (Cottingham & Warner, 1978, p. 604).

Shortly thereafter in 1975 AACD appointed a special Licensure Commission with Thomas J. Sweeney of Ohio University as its first chairperson. The commission was initially formed to give AACD a sense of direct responsibility and leadership in reacting to increasing counselor concerns about credentialing and licensure. The commission had essentially three tasks: (a) to collect and disseminate information about licensure developments at the state and national level, (b) to assist members and state groups to resolve licensure problems at the legislative or examining board level, and (c) to provide leadership for counselors in seeking relationships with other professional groups, state and local governmental agencies, and state legislatures (Cottingham & Warner, 1978). The basic philosophy of the commission was to develop policies that would enable the profession to change from a reactive to an proactive stance in pursuit of counselor licensing. In January 1976 the commission widely distributed an action packet, which included an "Overview of Counselor Licensure" containing strategies for state and regional AACD groups to use in pursuing licensing. Also distributed in that packet was the fourth draft of model state legislation by the commission (APGA, 1974). Counselors were encouraged to evaluate the recommendations in the draft so that the commission could prepare a final revision for AACD approval.

By 1978 the commission had established a national licensure network of state representatives and a schedule of regional and state workshops on licensing as well as dialogues on credentialing with Division 17 of APA, the American Association of Marriage and Family Counselors, and the National Association of Social Workers (NASW). Also, the commission had started to study and develop a national register for counselors, a third-party payment bill for submission to Congress, and a formal procedure for gathering data and handling unfair action by licensure boards.

The commission, retitled the Licensure Committee, published a *Licensure Committee Action Packet* (APGA, 1979), which was widely distributed and made available to members. Fretz and Mills (1980) viewed the packet as the "most thorough set of preparatory materials that any professional organization of counseling or psychologists has made available to its members" (p. 84). The packet contained a rationale for support of counselor licensure and model legislation for states. Licensing the practice of counseling and protection for the title "Licensed Professional Counselor" were recommended. The title was "restricted to any person who holds himself/herself out to the public by any title or description of services incorporating the words 'licensed professional counselor'; and who offers to render professional counseling services to individuals, groups, organizations, corporations, institutions, governmental agencies or the public for a fee, monetary or otherwise, implying that s/he is licensed and trained, experienced or expert in counseling, and who holds a current, valid license to practice counseling" (APGA, 1979, p. 23). The practice of counseling was defined as including but not limited to the five areas of counseling: appraisal activities, consulting, referral activities, and research activities. A definition for each "practice" area was given.

The recommended standard for education was the master's degree from a regionally accredited institution, with the qualification that the degree be primarily counseling in content and would meet the academic and training standards established by the board. Use of standards such as the AACD "Standards for the Preparation of Counselors and Other Personnel Services Specialists" (AACD, 1977) were recommended for board adoption. Setting the master's degree as a minimum standard for licensing was in sharp contrast to the committee's 1976 recommendation for training, which listed a doctoral degree or a 60-semester-hour program as the standard for licensing.

For experience before licensing, the committee recommended 3 full years of supervised experience, 1 year of which could be obtained before the master's degree. Also, it was recommended that candidates demonstrate professional competency by passing a written and/or oral and/or performance examination prescribed by the board. In deviating from the generic licensing practices of psychologists, the committee recommended that an enabling clause be included in the legislation so boards would later make provisions for licensing specialty practice areas. The rational for that section included the acknowledgment that marriage and family and rehabilitation counselors were also seeking licensure legislation. In addition, another enabling clause was recommended that would provide provisions for other individuals (i.e., drug, alcohol, and rehabilitation counselors) to seek registration or certification in the future.

To maintain a license, a clause on continuing education was recommended, with the requirement that counselors every 2 years provide evidence of continued education acceptable to the board. The standard exclusion clauses for other professions, students, and the clergy were included in the model legislation. However, so as not to disenfranchise legitimate professionals who were providing services at the time, the committee recommended that the board be able to adopt provisions under a "grandfather clause" that would enable such persons to meet reasonable requirements for licensing established by the board. Also, a 5-year time period was recommended for individuals to practice under a limited associate license while pursuing the requirements set forth by the board.

Recommendations and specific wording for the other common aspects of licensing legislation, such as privileged communication, reciprocity, code of ethics and violations, and unlawful practice with penalties, were included by the committee. Although the supervision of counselors was mentioned, few specific directives were given. An important aspect of regulation and notification and protection of the public previously recommended by Gross (1977) was included in the recommendations by the committee: that counselors must provide a professional disclosure statement outlining their education, specialties, and other pertinent information for the client prior to providing services.

Association Efforts and Later Developments

In 1974 the Southern Association of Counselor Education and Supervision was the first AACD divisional unit to establish a licensure committee (Cottingham & Warner, 1978). The SACES Licensure Committee and the AACD Licensure Commission worked with the Virginia Association for Counseling and Development (previously VPGA) and Virginia Counselor Association for passage of the Virginia 1975 and 1976 licensing legislation (Swanson, 1988). In 1976 the Association of Counselor Education and Supervision appointed a Licensure Commission (Carroll, Griggs, & Halligan,

1977), and in 1977 the American School Counselors Association and AACD Licensure Committees held a joint workshop to train ASCA regional consultants to help states in their area pass licensing legislation (Cottingham & Warner, 1978). Special issues of the *Personnel and Guidance Journal* (now the *Journal of Counseling and Development*) on credentialing edited by Jerald Forster (1977, 1978) were used to inform the profession of the need for licensing and the various strategies that could be used. Assisted by ASCA, ACES, and AACD committees, the state associations in Arkansas and Alabama were able to successfully pass counselor licensing acts in 1979. As of 1979, 41 states had licensure committees, and 24 states had introduced licensure bills in their legislatures (Fretz & Mills, 1980). The American Mental Health Counselors Association began to award financial assistance grants to state organizations for licensing in 1980 and became actively involved in lobbying in Florida in 1981 (Brooks, 1986). Since that time AMHCA has contributed more funds to state organizations for passage of licensure legislation than any other AACD division. Texas and Florida passed counselor licensing legislation in 1981 and were followed by Idaho in 1982. North Carolina passed counselor regulations in 1983, and Ohio and Georgia passed counselor legislation in 1984. Six states passed counselor licensing acts in 1985, followed by three states in 1986, six states in 1987, and five states in 1988. Currently there are 35 states with counselor regulatory acts (Dingman, 1990).

Gerstein (1988) reviewed the counselor licensing acts passed from 1975 through 1987, and although he found a great variability in education requirements and some variability in experience requirements, almost all other sections of the statutes were highly consistent among the states. Academic requirements ranged from a master's degree requiring 30 semester hours to a graduate degree requiring 60 semester hours. The majority of states stipulated a master's degree with the specific number of semester hours to be determined by the board. Requirements for experience varied from 2 to 4 years (Brooks & Gerstein, 1990), but the vast majority of states required 2 years of supervised experience. The majority of states defined counseling procedures to include counseling, appraisal, consulting, and referral services to individuals, groups, and organizations. Three states did not define counseling procedures in their statutes. Four states by 1987 had included the requirement of professional disclosure within their acts. That type of regulation and protection of the public can be included in board rules created after the act is passed, and many states have done so. Ten boards regulating the practice of counseling in 1987 were omnibus boards that also regulated at least one other profession. With four of seven states passing counselor licensing acts in 1987 to include an omnibus board, Gerstein (1988) was prompted to conclude that counselors, marriage and family therapists, and social workers were collaborating in increasing efforts to attain licensure. Approximately half of the counselor licensure boards also regulate at least one other profession (Brooks & Gerstein, 1990). However, only two-thirds of those boards are omnibus boards, with the remaining boards having the capacity to grant specialty licenses.

The Influence of Accreditation Standards

Another means of providing accountability and quality control is program accreditation. Institutions of higher education elect to accept the accrediting agency's predetermined criteria or training standards as a means of showing programmatic and institutional quality. Accreditation is a voluntary process by an institution, and the accrediting group has no legal control over the institution (Dickey, 1968). However, although accreditation does not have the legal control of licensing regulations, it has been an extremely important factor in determining the status of professional groups and facilitating licensing efforts. All of the licensed professions in this country began the process of regulation and quality control by developing standards for training programs. Eventually, graduation from an accredited institution and program became a requirement for licensing.

The foremost contribution by ACES to the profession has been in the area of accreditation of programs. Accreditation was viewed by ACES members in the 1970s as equally—if not more—important to the profession than licensing (Sweeney, 1978). (See chapter 4 for the history of the accreditation movement in AACD.) Accreditation of counselor education programs was viewed as one of the necessary steps to insure counselor accountability and also to foster professional accountability through licensing (Sweeney & Witmer, 1977).

The ACES "Standards for the Preparation of Counselors and Other Personnel Services Specialists" (ACES, 1973) were highly effective in furthering the aims of the counselor licensure movement. The standards specified a common core of knowledge areas necessary for the preparation of all counselors and personnel service specialists. This common core consisted of (a) human growth and development, (b) social and cultural foundations, (c) the helping relationship, (d) groups, (e) life style and career development, (f) appraisal of the individual, (g) research and evaluation, and (h) professional orientation areas of study. Expectations and relevant courses of study for each area were specified. The core areas in the standards are unique among the mental health professions in defining the training required of the practitioner and are a means of distinguishing the counseling profession from all other mental health professions. Also included in the standards were guidelines to establish requirements for specialty areas above the core requirements.

Citing the ACES standards within licensing legislation to define the educational requirements for licensing was recommended within the 1976 draft of model legislation by the AACD Licensure Committee. The first few states that licensed counselors followed the recommendations and cited the standards as a guide for state boards to establish training requirements. By 1979 the standards had been approved by AACD and received more acknowledgement and wider distribution in the profession. The publicity given the standards and their recommendation for inclusion in licensing legislation within the 1979 *Licensure Committee Action Packet* motivated and enabled many states to specify the core areas as a requirement for training in their licensure acts. When written into licensure acts, the core areas can provide counselors additional protection for practice of their profession. The recommended wording within the exemption section of the prescribed model legislation adopted by APA states that members of other professions are not restricted "from rendering services consistent with their professional training or code of ethics" (APA, 1987, p. 700).

Including the educational requirements in the licensing act is also helpful in other ways. The recommended definition by the AACD Licensure Committee of counseling practice, which appears in most licensure acts, is not as all encompassing as that given by psychology. Counseling procedures are well defined, however, and they are given added significance by the inclusion of parallel training requirements. The three sections of counselor practice, counseling procedures, and professional training provide a comprehensive view of counseling that should be persuasive to legislators and judges that counseling is a specific profession.

The attempt to develop and implement training standards had other desirable effects on the counselor licensure movement. In 1977 the ACES membership approved the "Guidelines for Doctoral Preparation in Counselor Education" (Stripling, 1978). These guidelines together with the 1973 standards formed a comprehensive basis for agreement on requirements for counselor training. The adoption of the requirements by AACD and many divisions led to the establishment of the Council for Accreditation of Counseling and Related Educational Programs in 1981. In just 6 years CACREP was able to attain national recognition and approval by the Council on Postsecondary Accreditation (COPA) as a valid accrediting group in higher education. This recognition by COPA has further substantiated the credibility of counselor training and, more importantly, acknowledged that training as distinct among the social sciences. COPA will not approve groups that duplicate already existing (approved) disciplines or programs of study.

Based on the impetus and agreement on the ACES standards and doctoral guidelines, in a similar evolutionary development to CACREP, the National Board for Certified Counselors was established in 1982. The NBCC has set training standards, adopted the AACD Code of Ethics and continuing education requirements, and developed a national examination for certification. In 1985 NBCC was recognized by the National Commission for Certifying Agencies (NCCA), which is the foremost organizational recognition for national certification. As of 1990, NBCC has certified 17,300 counselors. National certification for counselors was originally proposed as an alternative means to licensing to protect counselors and enable the profession to gain national recognition. Except for the states without counselor licensure acts, those goals may have been fulfilled. National certification lacks the legal authority of state boards in regulating the profession, however.

NBCC has not only developed certification standards and procedures but has also put in years of study to develop a national examination for practitioners. Validation of that examination occurred at the time when most states had passed their licensing acts and were writing their governance rules. That was fortunate for the profession because the development of professional examinations is very costly, and the examinations have often been challenged in the courts. Almost all state counselor licensure boards contract with NBCC to use that examination in their states.

Recent Developments in the Counselor Licensure Movement

In a relatively short time span, from 1981 to 1986, state legislatures in 15 states passed counselor licensing acts. New boards had to be formed, and board rules and regulations for administering the acts needed to be written. Based on requests for information and aid from newly formed state boards, the AACD Licensure Committee in the spring of 1986 established a committee to develop plans to create an association of state licensing boards. Representatives from several state boards met in the fall of 1986 and formed the American Association of State Counseling Boards (AASCB) (Dingman, Swanson, Brooks, & Schmitz, 1988). The purposes of the board include (a) facilitating communication among member boards, (b) encouraging collaborative efforts in developing compatible standards and procedures for regulation, (c) setting forth opinions of the association in serving to protect the public and communicating those opinions to governmental bodies and association groups, (d) providing assistance to member boards to fulfill statutory, professional, public, and ethical obligations in legal regulation and enforcement, and (e) engaging in and encouraging research into matters related to the legal regulation of counseling. In addition to state board membership, AASCB has organizational affiliates that include ACES, AMHCA, ASCA, the National Academy of Certified Clinical Mental Health Counselors, NBCC, and the National Career Development Association. Including the affiliates in board activities enables input by those organizations and also enables AASCB to utilize many of the resources of the affiliate organizations. An example of collaborate efforts and mutual assistance is the AASCB-recommended adoption of the NBCC examination by states for licensing counselors.

Since 1977 the AACD Licensure Committee has recommended supervised clinical experience as a prerequisite for obtaining a license (Brooks & Gerstein, 1990). However, the model legislation and commentary published by the committee does not include specifics about the supervision process or roles of the supervisor. State boards have been left to their own resources to determine those rules and regulations. Acknowledging this absence and the need for supervision standards, the ACES Supervision Network, under the direction of L. DiAnne Borders and Allan Dye, drafted a set of supervision standards that were revised and approved in 1988 by the ad hoc AACD Interdivisional Task Force on Supervision Credentialing. In 1989 the ACES "Standards for Counseling Supervisors" (ACES, 1989) were adopted by AACD and also approved by AASCB for incorporation into state board rules and regulations governing supervision. These standards specify 11 core areas of knowledge, skills, and traits of effective supervisors along with competencies for supervisors and expectations of counselors. Recommendations for the education and training of supervisors are also included within the standards. In order to fill some segments of the supervised experience that lack national guidelines, the ACES Supervision Network in 1989 developed "Ethical Standards for Counseling Supervisors" (ACES, 1990). Although these ethical standards may need some revision before adoption by AACD and AASCB, they represent, together with the standards for supervisors, a highly comprehensive set of regulations for supervisor, supervisee, and client interrelationships.

Other Groups Seeking Licensure

Although the counselor licensure movement was in its infancy from 1974 to 1979, seven states had already passed legislation regulating marriage and family therapy. Three of the seven states passed their regulations during the 1960s. An extremely hard fought battle was waged between mental health counselors and marriage and family therapists in Georgia in 1978 over the "sunset" of the marriage and family therapist regulations (Brooks, 1986). The abolishment of the Georgia statute and the aggressiveness of counselors caused the American Association for Marriage and Family Therapy in 1979 to take a proactive stance in supporting state legislation and in defining acceptable legislation for marriage and family therapists (Everett, 1990). AAMFT was established in 1942 as the American Association of Marriage Counselors. The association has developed specific training criteria for each level of membership in the association, which includes an approved supervisor status. In 1978, AAMFT's Commission on Accreditation was formally recognized by the U.S. Department of Health, Education, and Welfare as the national accreditation agency for graduate degree programs and postdegree training centers for marriage and family therapy. AAMFT views marriage and family therapy as a unique and distinct discipline and has been actively involved in collaborating with AACD and CACREP on licensure and accreditation issues. These collaborative efforts, at least for the short term, may have reached an impasse. In 1990 the International Association of Marriage and Family Counseling was approved as a new division of AACD. Following that approval, preliminary standards for accreditation of marriage and family counselor training programs were adopted by CACREP. CACREP has been recognized by the Council on Postsecondary Accreditation, and COPA recognizes only one group for each accreditation area. Thus, AAMFT may have difficulty in attaining recognition by COPA. To further this conflict, marriage and family therapists are deeply concerned over the statutory ability of some state counselor licensing boards to add specialty provisions or licenses to their control of the field. Everett (1990) cites the actions of the Maryland Counselors' Board in subsuming the practice of marriage and family under the counseling field as unacceptable to marriage and family therapists. AACD and state counselor associations, however, have the opportunity to treat the field of marriage and family therapy in an equitable manner. Since 1979, 15 state legislatures have passed licensure or certification acts in marriage and family therapy. Seven of those acts created omnibus boards to include both counselors and marriage and family therapists. Thus, the potential for collaborative efforts and agreement exists for both groups.

Rehabilitation counselors have also been concerned about being excluded from counselor licensing acts and about losing the power of self-regulation. Specifically, in an attempt to assert control over their profession, rehabilitation counselors in New Hampshire with the help of the National Rehabilitation Association in 1979 passed the first rehabilitation counselors licensing act. Many rehabilitation counselors have worked in the private sector and for insurance companies in the 1970s and throughout the 1980s. Differences in specialty and objectives of practice and, in some cases, training in comparison to mental health counselors were a source of concern. The Council on Rehabilitation Education, formed in 1971, is a member of the National Commission for Health Certifying Agencies (NCHCA) and accredits graduate and undergraduate rehabilitation training programs. The graduate program standards of CORE and COPA are very similar (Hosie, Patterson, & Hollingsworth, 1989). Differences exist, as would be expected in program requirements because of the specialization denoted by rehabilitation counseling. Those differences, however, are similar to the differences that exist among the specialty areas accredited by CACREP. The major difference is that CORE accredits undergraduate programs. Many graduates from bachelor's level programs work in private rehabilitation services, and they and their employers do not want counselor licensure acts to disenfranchise them. Most counselor licensure statutes contain the means to satisfy the needs of rehabilitation counselors, for example. grandfathering rules, specialty designations, and associate status. Five different professional organizations comprise CORE and represent the rehabilitation field. Only one of those groups, the American Rehabilitation Counselors Association, is affiliated with AACD, which sponsors the counselor licensure movement. Thus, there will probably be continued tensions for some time.

Sunset Legislation

Approximately three-quarters of the states have statutes that require periodic review of state licensure boards. These sunset regulations were instituted to insure that the needs of the public are met in the most efficient and cost-effective manner possible by state government. Fretz and Mills (1980) describe several forms of sunset regulations, which include (a) a periodic, "zero based" review of the need for the regulatory law, (b) specification of a date by which the legislation will terminate unless specifically confirmed by the legislature, and (c) the establishment of a termination date in the wake of a negative "fitness" finding. There are a number of examples of nonrenewal of psychology licensure statutes in the 1970s. In 1979 counselors and those with master's degrees in psychology combined forces to stop renewal of the Florida psychology licensing act. Now counselors may find themselves in a similar position because of opposition from other groups.

Issues and Implications for the Future

Licensure provides rules and regulations that determine who can be licensed and what procedures those who are licensed can practice. There is, however, a weak link between licensing and competency of practice (Danish & Smyer, 1981; Gross, 1978; Hogan, 1982; Spivack, 1984). In an attempt to regulate the quality of services of psychologists, state psychological associations have organized professional standards review committees (PSRCs) (Meltzer, 1975). Creating similar structures for review of professional practices may be helpful to counselors in insuring consumer protection and regulating services. Psychologists primarily organized PSRCs based on physicians' standards review committees, which are required by federal regulations to cover services to medicare patients (Young, 1982). Insurance companies and consumers commonly ask the review committee to render opinions as to whether a particular method or practice is usual, customary, or reasonable and as to what fees are appropriate (Fretz & Mills, 1980). Licensure boards usually consider only the ethical conduct of practitioners in providing services and do not intervene in other types of complaints. PSRCs can fill that type of void and also exert some control over quality of services and the fees charged. PSRCs review requests and complaints and, when appropriate, interview the practitioner involved. Clients' rights of privacy are maintained by the committee. After deliberation the committee provides a written judgment. Most committees allow appeals and have well-established appeal procedures. Instituting PSRCs will be especially important to counselors in pursuing third-party payments. Insurance companies want to know that the services provided are appropriate in terms of length of treatment and cost.

The counseling profession supports licensure for both master's- and doctoral-level graduates. There are also accreditation (CACREP) standards for both levels of training programs. Having two levels of preparation and granting each level equal status is unique in the major mental health professions. APA does not accredit master's degree programs in psychology, and although there are over 84,000 master's-level psychologists, only three states grant master's-level psychologists a full license (Dale, 1988). Social work grants equal status to both levels for the practice of the profession in licensure statutes. However, there are very few social work doctoral programs and no accreditation standards for those programs. There are no distinctive regulations acknowledging the different training levels in psychology and social work. Thus, the counseling profession is on its own in creating a system to utilize both levels of training effectively. Licensing both master's- and doctoral-level counselors is the single most important reason for the success of the counselor licensure movement. Yet the profession may still have to contend with the existence of two training levels.

The AACD Licensure Committee (AACD, 1989) recommends a master's degree with 60 semester hours as the minimum training standard for licensing. Forty-eight of the 60 semester hours are to be completed in at least eight of the nine core areas stipulated by ACES and CACREP. A minimum standard of 60 semester hours was first proposed by the Licensure Committee in 1976. AACD did not adopt that standard and instead adopted the recommended standard of a master's degree for licensing in 1979. As most states require a master's degree with less than 60 credit hours and CACREP requires a 48-hour program for most types of programs, it will be some time before the 60-hour requirement becomes universal in counselor training. Also, until more counselor education departments create 60-hour master's programs, there is little reason for state boards to require that standard for training. Perhaps an incentive to adopt the 60-hour-program requirement may come from CACREP, which has begun a self-mandated review of the training standards (1990 through 1993) and will publish a revised set of standards in 1994. CACREP may extend the requirements for master's-level training to 60 semester hours. If that is done, there will be an increase in the number of 60-hour master's programs, and that increase will affect the judgment of licensure boards to adopt that standard.

Acceptance of the 60-semester-hour standard for master's-level training by counselor education programs will have far reaching effects on doctoral training programs. As the number of credit hours for the master's increases and begins to consume what was previously part of the doctoral curriculum, the profession may have to reconceptualize doctoral training. The needs to differentiate master's- and doctoral-level practitioner roles and also to expand doctoral training into other areas are not new ideas in counselor education (Brown, 1989; Wilson, 1989). Some additional areas might include research, supervision, and management within agencies in the private and public sectors. The current proponents of 60-hour master's training programs appear to be interested in upgrading the profession and replacing the current standards in training for master's programs in counseling throughout the country. Irrespective of the designs for further changes in requirements for master's programs, such changes will force counselor educators to reassess the role and training for doctoral programs.

In the future, there will also be changes in licensure legislation and rules and regulations for counselor supervision. There are few guidelines from the other professions that counselors can use to develop supervision regulations. The ACES "Standards for Counseling Supervisors" (ACES, 1989) are very specific in describing the training needed by supervisors. State boards, depending on their needs, will adopt variations of those standards for supervisors. However, the standards appear to be more applicable to supervisors in counselor education programs, and state boards still have to contend with developing specific regulations for field supervision. In many states there are too few counselor educators to meet the demands of supervising new graduates who seek licensing. Previously there has been little demand for supervision because most counselors were licensed during the grandfathering period of the statute. Traditionally, master's-level training programs do not include courses on supervision. Thus, many state boards will need to develop training systems so that master's-level counselors can become proficient as supervisors. Those systems will need to contain suitable rewards so that counselors will participate and meet the state's demand for supervisors.

In conclusion, the AACD-recommended rules and regulations for counselor licensure acts form the most comprehensive set of regulations of any of the mental health professions. What remains for the profession is the creation of a viable and equitable system for implementation of those regulations. Unfortunately, expanding or changing the counselor licensing regulations will not produce licensure in states where it does not exist. Counselors will attain licensure in those states by obtaining increased public recognition and notoriety and through increased lobbying efforts. Fortunately, the AACD Licensure Committee's recommendations for regulations governing the profession allow for other mental health groups to merge with the counselor licensure movement, or at least form specialty designations. Working with other groups in combined efforts to enact licensure legislation will be extremely important in continuing the success of the counselor licensing movement.

References

American Association for Counseling and Development. (1989). *Model licensure bill for licensed professional counselors.* Alexandria, VA: Author.

American Association for Counseling and Development. (1977). *Standards for the preparation of counselors and other personnel services specialists.* Alexandria, VA: Author.

American Personnel and Guidance Association. (1976). *Model for state legislation concerning the practice of counseling, 1976, draft no. 4.* Alexandria, VA: Author.

American Personnel and Guidance Association. (1979). *Licensure Committee Action Packet.* Alexandria, VA: Author.

American Psychological Association. (1967). A model for state legislation affecting the practice of psychology 1967: Report of APA Committee on Legislation. *American Psychologist, 22,* 1095–1103.

American Psychological Association. (1987). Model act for state licensure of psychologists. *American Psychologist, 42,* 696–703.

Angel, J.L. (1970). *Directory of professional and occupational licensing in the United States.* New York: World Trade Academy.

Association for Counselor Education and Supervision. (1973). *Standards for the preparation of counselors and other personnel services specialists.* Alexandria, VA: American Association for Counseling and Development.

Association for Counselor Education and Supervision. (1978). Guidelines for doctoral preparation in counselor education. *Counselor Education and Supervision, 17,* 163–166.

Association for Counselor Education and Supervision. (1989, Spring). Standards for counseling supervisors. *ACES Spectrum,* 8–10.

Association for Counselor Education and Supervision. (1989). *Standards for counseling supervisors.* Alexandria, VA: American Association for Counseling and Development.

Association for Counselor Education and Supervision. (1990, Spring). Ethical standards for counseling supervisors. *ACES Spectrum,* 13–15.

Barber, R. (1965). Some problems in the sociology of professions. In K. Lynn (Ed.), *The Professions in America.* Boston: Houghton Mifflin.

Belcher, D. (1973). *A survey of counselor certification standards and counselor participation in certification practices.* Unpublished doctoral dissertation, Auburn University, Auburn, NY, DED B4273 c.2.

Bernstein, B.J., & Lecomte, C. (1981). Licensure in psychology: Alternative directions. *Professional Psychology, 12,* 200–208.

Brooks, D.K., Jr. (1986). Credentialing of mental health counselors. In A.J. Palmo & W.J. Weikel (Eds.), *Foundations of mental health counseling* (pp. 243–261). Springfield, IL: Charles C. Thomas.

Brooks, D.K., Jr., & Gerstein, L.H. (1990). Counselor credentialing and interprofessional collaboration. *Journal of Counseling and Development, 68,* 477–484.

Brown, D. (1989, Spring). Call for manuscripts. *ACES Spectrum,* 16.

Carman, H.J. (1958). The historical development of licensing for the profession. *The Educational Record, 39*(3), 268–278.

Carroll, M.R., Griggs, S.A., & Halligan, F.G. (1977). The licensure issue: How real is it? *Personnel and Guidance Journal, 55,* 577–580.

Cohen, H.S., & Miike, L.H. (1973). *Developments in health manpower licensure: A follow-up to the 1971 report on licensure and related health personnel credentialing* (Publication No. [HRA]74-3103). Washington, DC: U.S. Department of Health, Education, and Welfare.

Cottingham, H.F., & Warner, R.W., Jr. (1978). APGA and counselor licensure: A status report. *Personnel and Guidance Journal, 56,* 604.

Cummings, N.A. (1990). The credentialing of professional psychologists and its implication for the other mental health disciplines. *Journal of Counseling and Development, 68,* 485–490.

Dale, R.H.I. (1988). State psychological associations, licensing criteria, and the "master's issue." *Professional Psychology, 19,* 589–593.

Danish, S.J., & Smyer, M.A. (1981). Unintended consequences of requiring a license to help. *American Psychologist, 36,* 13–21.

Dickey, F.G. (1968). What is accrediting and why is it important for professional organizations? *Counselor Education and Supervision, 11,* 194–199.

Dingman, R.L. (1990, November). *American Association of State Counseling Boards: Counselor credentialing laws.* Paper presented at the Annual Conference of the Southern Association of Counselor Education and Supervision, Norfolk, VA.

Dingman, R.L., Swanson, C., Brooks, D., & Schmitz, D. (1988). The American Association of State Counseling Boards: An important resource. In R. Dingman (Ed.), *Licensure for mental health counselors* (pp. 39–43). Alexandria, VA: American Mental Health Counselors Association.

Ehrenreich, B., & English, D. (1973). *Witches, midwives, and nurses: A history of women healers.* Old Westbury, NY: Feminist Press.

Elliott, P. (1972). *The sociology of the professions.* New York: Macmillan.

Everett, C.A. (1990). The field of marital and family therapy. *Journal of Counseling and Development, 68,* 498–502.

Forster, J.R. (Ed.). (1977). Licensure/certification for counseling psychologists and counselors [Special issue]. *Personnel and Guidance Journal, 55*(10), 571–601.

Forster, J.R. (Ed.). (1978). Counselor credentialing update [Special issue]. *Personnel and Guidance Journal, 56*(10), 593–611.

Fretz, B.R., & Mills, D.H. (1980). *Licensing and certification of psychologists and counselors: A guide to current policies, procedures, and legislation.* San Francisco: Jossey-Bass.

Garcia, A. (1990). An examination of the social work profession's efforts to achieve legal regulation. *Journal of Counseling and Development, 68,* 491–497.

Gerstein, L. (1988). Current counselor credentialing laws and some thoughts about future model legislation. In R. Dingman (Ed.), *Licensure for mental health counselors* (pp. 8–21). Alexandria, VA: American Mental Health Counselors Association.

Gerstle, J., & Jacobs, G. (Eds.). (1976). *Professions for the people.* Cambridge, MA: Schenkman.

Goode, W.J. (1960). Encroachment, charlatanism, and the emerging professions: Psychology, sociology, and medicine. *American Sociological Review, 25,* 902–914.

Gross, S.J. (1977). Professional disclosure: An alternative to licensing. *Personnel and Guidance Journal, 55,* 586–588.

Gross, S.J. (1978). The myth of professional licensing. *American Psychologist, 33,* 1109–1016.

Hogan, D.B. (1982). When little is known, what are we to do? The implications of social science research. *Professional Practice of Psychology, 3,* 19–25.

Hosie, T.W., Patterson, J.B., & Hollingsworth, D. (1989). School and rehabilitation counselor preparation: Meeting the needs of individuals with disabilities. *Journal of Counseling and Development, 68,* 171–176.

Kiesler, C.A., & Zaro, S.J. (1981). The development of psychology as a profession in the United States. *International Review of Applied Psychology, 30,* 341–353.

Mack, G.L. (1982). The governance of nonmedical mental health occupations. (Doctoral dissertation, University of Georgia, 1981). *Dissertation Abstracts International, 43*(10–A), 4302.

Meltzer, M.L. (1975). Insurance reimbursement: A mixed blessing. *American Psychologist, 30,* 1150–1156.

Pavalko, R. (1971). *Sociology of occupations and professions.* Itasca, IL: Peacock.

Shryock, R.H. (1967). *Medical licensing in America, 1650–1965.* Baltimore, MD: Johns Hopkins University Press.

Spector, S., & Frederick, W. (1952). *A study of state legislation licensing the practice of professions and other occupations.* Chicago: Council of State Governments.

Spivack, J.D. (1984). Animals at the crossroads: A prospective on credentialing in the mental health field. *The Counseling Psychologist, 12* (4), 175–182.

Stripling, R.O. (1978). Standards and accreditation in counselor education: A proposal. *Personnel and Guidance Journal, 56,* 608–611.

Swanson, C. (1988). Historical perspective on licensure for counselors. In R.L. Dingman (Ed.), *Licensure for mental health counselors* (pp. 1–3). Alexandria, VA: American Mental Health Counselors Association.

Sweeney, T.J. (1978). Counselor credentialing: Promises and pitfalls. *Viewpoints in Teaching and Learning, 54* (1) 56–63.

Sweeney, T.J., & Sturdevant, A.D. (1974). Licensure in the helping professions: Anatomy of an issue. *Personnel and Guidance Journal, 52,* 575–580.

Sweeney, T.J., & Witmer, J.M. (1977). Who says you're a counselor? *Personnel and Guidance Journal, 55,* 589–594.

Tabachnik, L. (1976). Licensing in the legal and medical professions, 1820–1860: A historical case study. In J. Gerstle & G. Jacobs (Eds.), *Professions for the people.* Cambridge, MA: Schenkman.

U.S. Department of Health, Education and Welfare. (1971). *Report on licensure and related health personnel credentialing* (Publication No. [HMS]72–11). Washington, DC: Government Printing Office.

Wilson, F.R. (1989, Fall). Resources and research network call for proposals. *ACES Spectrum,* 5.

Young, H.H. (1982). A brief history of quality assurance and peer review. *Professional Psychology, 13,* 9–13.

CHAPTER 4

Accreditation in Counselor Education

Michael K. Altekruse and Joe Wittmer

Introduction and Background

Accreditation is a process whereby an association or agency grants public recognition to a school, institute, college, university, or specialized program of study that has met certain established qualifications or standards as determined through initial and periodic evaluations. In the case of counselor education, accreditation is currently granted by an affiliate of the American Association for Counseling and Development: the Council for Accreditation of Counseling and Related Educational Programs or CACREP.

This official accrediting body for the American Association for Counseling and Development was incorporated in 1981 and gained recognition from the Council on Postsecondary Accreditation in 1987 (CACREP, 1988).

The standards or evaluative criteria utilized in the accreditation process have a long history in the counseling profession. An organized movement to establish standards for development and evaluation of counselor education programs began in 1960. A joint committee of the Association for Counselor Education and Supervision and the American School Counselors Association helped organize two massive studies, which took over 5 years to complete and involved over 700 counselor educators and supervisors and more than 2,500 practicing counselors (Stripling & Dugan, 1961).

These two studies aided greatly in the initial development of the first official standards in counselor education in 1964. The "Standards for Counselor Education in the Preparation of Secondary School Counselors" (ACES, 1964) were utilized on a trial basis for 3 years and then officially adopted by ACES in 1967 (ACES, 1967). At the same time a manual for self-study was developed to assist programs in complying with the new standards (APGA, 1967).

In addition to the 1967 standards, the "Standards for Preparation of Elementary School Counselors" (APGA, 1968) were established in 1968. Subsequently, in 1969 the "Guidelines for Graduate Programs in the

Preparation of Student Personnel Workers in Higher Education" (APGA, 1969) were developed. In 1973 these three sets of standards were rewritten and combined into the "Standards for the Preparation of Counselors and Other Personnel Services Specialists" (ACES, 1973). The standards were adopted by ACES in 1973, by ASCA in 1977, and by the American Personnel and Guidance Association in 1977. Also approved by ACES in 1977 were the "Guidelines for Doctoral Preparation in Counselor Education" (Altekruse & Karmos, 1979). However, until 1979 these standards were not used for official accreditation decisions, with the exception of a variation used for state approval in the state of Wisconsin (1972) and state accreditation by California ACES (1973) (Altekruse & Karmos, 1979). Then, in 1979, the standards were used by the ACES National Committee on Accreditation in accrediting programs on a pilot basis. Minor changes in the standards were made by the ACES committee during this stage. The ACES committee also agreed to accept all of California's ACES previous accreditation decisions (five programs), provided it ceased accrediting counselor preparation programs. This left ACES as the only association accrediting body using the standards of training. In 1981, the APGA Board of Directors adopted a resolution to gain control formally over the responsibilities of the ACES accrediting body. With this action, CACREP was officially formed as an independent accrediting body sponsored by APGA/AACD and several participating divisions (CACREP, 1987).

CACREP adopted the existing standards at its first meeting in September 1981. Although the first few years of CACREP brought about many suggested changes in the preparation standards (CACREP, 1982, 1987), a moratorium was declared for a 5-year period in which only minor changes would be permitted. The 5-year period ended in 1986 when the first major changes since the inception of the standards were introduced by CACREP. The "new" standards became the official standards of CACREP on July 1, 1988, and will remain so until July 1, 1993.

Advantages of Accreditation

The 1988 *Accreditation Procedures Manual and Application* (CACREP, 1988) lists the advantages of accreditation to the public, to students, to institutions of higher education, and to the profession and reveals how all are better served when preparation programs adhere to training standards. In addition to these advantages, many others are now evident. For example, graduates of non-CACREP-approved programs must receive 2 years of supervised experience as practicing counselors before they are eligible to become nationally certified counselors; however, students in a CACREP-approved counselor training program may take the National Counselor

Examination (NCE) in their last semester of training and upon graduation become nationally certified counselors.

In many states graduates of CACREP-approved programs also have advantages in state school counselor certification and in licensure as professional counselors. Some states only certify school counselors who have graduated from a CACREP or equivalent program. Maryland and Illinois are two such states. Licensure laws often specify the type of program applicants have to complete and in so doing often describe CACREP-equivalent programs.

The National Council for Accreditation of Teacher Education long accredited entry-level programs in school counseling as it evaluated schools of education. NCATE has been approved by the Council on Postsecondary Accreditation, as has CACREP. NCATE continues to accredit schools of education and will examine school counseling programs. CACREP-approved programs, however, do not have to go through the NCATE process because NCATE accepts CACREP decisions.

The Accreditation Process

Institutions make application to the executive director of CACREP. A major component of this application is a detailed self-study comparing the institution's program and specialities to the CACREP standards. Independent raters from CACREP evaluate the self-study against the standards and make specific recommendations to the CACREP's executive director. The executive director compiles these observations and shares them with the applicant institution. The applicant institution answers all queries from the executive director. If at this point a decision is made to conduct an on-site visitation, members of the visiting team are chosen by the applicant institution from a list supplied by the executive director. All documents are sent to the visiting team members and the visit arranged. The on-site team visits the institution (usually for 2½ to 3 days), compares the standards to all aspects of the program, and then makes a written detailed report to CACREP. This report is shared with the applicant institution by the executive director. The institution is provided the opportunity to answer and possibly rebuke the team's report in a written response to the CACREP executive director. All documents, including the self-study, all correspondence, and the team report, are then examined by a subcommittee of CACREP. This subcommittee makes specific recommendation to the CACREP board, which in turn makes accreditation decisions regarding the applicant's programs. The institution's highest designated administrator is informed in writing of CACREP's accreditation decisions.

Changes in the Standards

Length of the Programs

The desired length of the entry-level preparation programs in counseling has been debated for more than 20 years. Most agree that a minimum of 2 years is needed to train a counselor. Early training standards basically addressed the training of school counselors and called for a 1-year training program. As the field of counseling became broader and counselor programs began training professionals for additional settings, the length of training needed became an issue.

One of the first changes made by the ACES Committee on Accreditation in 1978 was that an entry-level program needed to be 2 years in length as defined by the minimum full-time student load at the institution's graduate school. If a particular graduate school defined a minimum full-time load as 9 semester hours per student, then a 2-year program for that institution would be 36 semester hours, consisting of four semesters of 9 hours each. Because this varied from institution to institution (one institution stated that a full-time load for a graduate student was 6 semester hours), CACREP changed this requirement to 2 full academic years of graduate study, defined as a 72-quarter-hour/48-semester-hour program, as a minimum prior to an on-site visit. However, the mental health CACREP counseling specialty requires 60 semester hours or 90 quarter hours as a minimum for CACREP accreditation.

Common Core

The eight areas of the CACREP common core standards have basically remained the same since the beginning of accreditation activities. An institution does not have to have to have a specific course for covering the content of each area of the common core. However, a curricular experience covering each common core is required. The faculty must show that each common core area is successfully integrated or infused in the curriculum and adequately covered. The core is required for every student enrolled in the entry-level program specialities of school counseling, community counseling, student affairs (counseling), mental health counseling, and the new marriage and family counseling. A somewhat different core of curricular experiences is required for student affairs (developmental and administrative).

The new standards define each common area more clearly and specifically and should make the integration or infusion approach much easier for counseling faculty.

Environmental and Specialty Standards

Many specialty groups have desired to have their specific standards included in the appendices of the CACREP manual as environmental or specialty standards, that is, as an official CACREP specialty area. Presently, there are four CACREP entry-level master's-level specialty areas (with one pending). These are as follows:

1. Community counseling
2. Mental health counseling
3. School counseling
4. Student affairs practice in higher education
   a. Counseling
   b. Developmental
   c. Administrative
5. Marriage and family counseling (pending).

There is also one doctoral specialty area (counselor education and supervision).

During the March 1990 CACREP board meeting, the specialty area of marriage and family counseling was accepted for review for possible inclusion. Member institutions (approved CACREP programs) and members of CACREP (divisions and AACD) will review the marriage and family standards and will vote on the approval or disapproval of marriage and family counseling as a specialty area.

Each of the specialty programs requires different standards of preparation with varying requirements. An institution is obligated to meet the basic generic CACREP standards in order to receive accreditation plus the environmental and specialty standards of their choice. Institutions were required to meet the specialty standards under the "old" standards, but the newer specialty standards have changed dramatically. The specialty standards are now more specific in terms of requirements, with the one exception of the more generic community counseling specialty area. However, the authors predict that the latter specialty area will change dramatically during the current revision of the standards.

Faculty

CACREP has long debated the number of faculty needed to staff the various specialities adequately. The old standards required a designated leader plus additional staff at the ratio of one faculty for every 10 FTE graduate students or the equivalent. The manual also indicated that two full-time counselor education members were needed for a doctoral preparation program. Since this standard was somewhat vague and did not really address the needs of the different program specialties, the new standards were changed to increase clarity and specificity.

The 1988 standards require at least three full-time faculty members be assigned to the academic unit in counselor education. One must be the designated leader of the program, with an additional faculty member identified as the program leader for each specialty program area being reviewed. Also, two additional faculty members should be teaching in each specialty program area under CACREP review.

Supervised Experiences

The first and most obvious change in the newer CACREP standards is the title of this area, which is now termed *clinical instruction*. In the old standards this area left much to interpretation and caused confusion among concerned professionals. The new standards attempt to clear up any confusion so that each program under CACREP review can more specifically meet this important training area. However, there are still parts of the clinical instruction area open to interpretation and confusion that bring about much debate among counselor educators and others.

The standards have changed from a specific hour requirement to a somewhat confusing *recommended* hour requirement to specific hour requirements in clinical instruction. A practicum student must spend a minimum 100 clock hours in practicum activities of which 40 hours should be in direct service work with appropriate clientele. One hour a week in individual supervision and 1½ hours a week should be in direct service work with appropriate clientele. One hour a week in individual supervision and 1½ hours a week in group supervision are required and counted within the minimum 100 clock hours of practicum activities.

The internship requirement is now 600 clock hours, 240 of which should be in direct service. A student may also count the 1 hour a week of individual supervision and the 1½ hours a week of group supervision within the 600-hour requirement. Practicum and internship requirements for the mental health counseling specialty consist of at least 1,000 clock hours of supervised experience in the appropriate setting under the direct supervision of a Certified Clinical Mental Health Counselor or other appropriate credentialed mental health professional.

The original CACREP standards called for doctoral students to have only 1 academic year (36 weeks) of full-time internship, and this included the one term of internship taken during the student's respective entry-level program of studies. The 1988 standards require two doctoral-level internships of 600 clock hours each. The supervision of five students individually in entry-level and doctoral-level practicums and internships is considered equivalent to a 3-semester-hour class. However, a practicum or internship seminar may consist of up to 10 students. This whole area is considered confusing to many and requires interpretation. The old standards called for a 5:1 student-supervisor ratio.

In the 1988 standards, CACREP also encourages students to acquire liability insurance prior to enrolling in practicum or internship.

Other Ratios

CACREP calls for the ratio of FTE students to FTE faculty to be no greater than 10:1, the same ratio as presented in the past. And, as in the earlier standards, one paid graduate assistantship is required to be available for every 30 FTE students.

Student-to-adviser ratios have been added to the 1988 CACREP standards. An entry-level adviser may advise up to 20 students, whereas at the doctorate level, a faculty member may chair 10 doctoral committees and serve on an additional 10 doctoral committees.

The clerical help requirement in the past was both confusing and liberal. A program was required to have one full-time secretary plus additional help at the ratio of one full-time clerical assistant for the equivalent of three faculty members. The 1988 standards require one FTE secretary for every five FTE faculty members.

Use of Computers

The use of computers was implied in the earlier CACREP standards but not explicitly stated. In the 1988 standards the requirements for faculty and students concerning the use of computers for word processing, data analysis, and research are much clearer.

Accreditation Decisions

The original categories established by the ACES National Committee on Accreditation and adopted by CACREP included:

- full accreditation (7 years)
- provisional with commendation (2 years for programs without graduates)
- provisional with recommendation (2 years)
- denied.

The 1988 categories include:

- accreditation (7 years)
- accreditation (2 to 4 years)
- denied.

Programs should have at least five graduates from any new or changed program before an on-site visit can be conducted.

Accreditation Fees

When accreditation began, the institution paid an up-front application fee plus all expenses incurred by the three members of the on-site visitation team. There were no annual fees. Presently, the institution pays a $600 application fee, a set fee covering the expense of the on-site visit ($3,000 for three-member teams and $4,000 for four), and upon receiving accreditation an annual $150 fee per specialty program accredited.

Doctoral Standards

The doctoral standards were designed and developed to supplement the entry-level standards. Students who enter a CACREP doctoral program should have graduated from a CACREP entry-level program or its equivalent, or make up the entry-level deficiencies during their doctoral preparation. Overall, the 1988 doctoral-level standards lack detail in certain areas and are open to criticism and considerable interpretation. The authors speculate that the 1993 standards for doctoral-level training will be greatly revised.

Related Accreditation Bodies

There are other accrediting bodies that accredit counselor education and/or former counselor education programs.

The National Council for Accreditation of Teacher Education, as discussed earlier, was for years the exclusive accrediting body for counselor education. Because 95% of counselor education programs were in departments or colleges of education, this was natural. However, with the movement toward more specialities in counselor education and with the NCATE limitation of accrediting programs related to the educational setting only (school counseling), NCATE became too restrictive for most counselor education programs. Presently, NCATE accepts CACREP accreditation decisions for school counseling programs.

The American Psychological Association accredits doctoral programs in counseling and clinical psychology. Many counselor education programs have chosen to change their name to counseling psychology and seek accreditation on the doctoral level through APA. Some of these programs have also sought CACREP accreditation on the master's or entry level. Like CACREP, APA is COPA approved.

The Committee on Accreditation for Marriage and Family Therapy Education (COAMFTE) accredits programs in marriage and family and is an affiliate of the American Association for Marriage and Family Therapy. At this writing AAMFT is not COPA approved. AACD accepted the International Association for Marriage and Family Counselors as a division in 1990, and CACREP tentatively approved standards for marriage and family counselors. AAMFT has seen the creation of IAMFC as competing with its organization. This competition has stimulated some discussion between the two groups.

The National Association of Social Workers is COPA approved and accredits programs in social work. The association utilizes an accrediting process with an on-site visit similar to CACREP's. However, NASW insists that a social work program be its own school of social work.

The American Rehabilitation Counseling Association, the National Rehabilitation Counseling Association, and the National Council on Rehabilitation Education formed an independent Council on Rehabilitation Education in 1971. CORE is COPA approved as an accrediting body and accredits rehabilitation counselor education programs. The accreditation process utilized by CORE is different from CACREP's in that on-site visits are usually not conducted. Verification of the self-study is accomplished through the mail and by telephone. Recently CORE and CACREP have made on-site visits together to counselor education programs that have a specialty in rehabilitation counseling. There is speculation that CORE and CACREP will cooperate even more in the future.

Summary

The standards of preparation for counselors were developed over 20 years ago as a response to ACES and ASCA members who were concerned about quality training for school counselors. Since that time the standards have been altered dramatically as the profession has changed and, in the opinion of the writers, will continue to change as the profession of counseling grows.

In 1986 CACREP rewrote the standards in an effort to clarify and more accurately describe current practice. The CACREP revision was presented to institutional CACREP members, CACREP board members, and AACD divisional representatives for critique and recommendations. ACES held workshops at each fall regional convention in an effort to receive maximum feedback in this revision stage. ACES then had a national workshop with a representative from each of the regional meetings. It was at this meeting that the final ACES revisions for the new CACREP standards were completed. These revisions were presented to CACREP in December 1986 for subcommittee consideration. CACREP made the final revisions based on maximum input from all parties involved at a special meeting of the CACREP board in spring 1987.

In 1990 both ACES and CACREP initiated a standards review process designed to revise the standards. These new standards will become effective July 1, 1993. ACES chose to utilize the same processes used in 1986 with two membership review processes (rather than the 1986 one-review process) conducted at regional ACES meetings in fall 1990 and 1991.

References

Altekruse, M., & Karmos, J. (1979). *Accreditation Training Manual*. Falls Church, VA: American Personnel and Guidance Association.

American Personnel and Guidance Association. (1967). *Manual for self-study by a counselor education staff*. Washington, DC: Author.

American Personnel and Guidance Association. (1968). *Standards for preparation of elementary school counselors*, Washington, DC: Author.

American Personnel and Guidance Association. (1969). *Guidelines for graduate programs in the preparation of student personnel workers in higher education*. Washington, DC: Author.

Association for Counselor Education and Supervision. (1964). Standards for counselor education in the preparation of secondary school counselors. *Personnel and Guidance Journal, 42,* 1060–1073.

Association for Counselor Education and Supervision. (1967). *Standards for the preparation of secondary school counselors*. Washington, DC: Author.

Association for Counselor Education and Supervision. (1973). *Standards for the preparation of counselors and other personnel service specialists*. Washington, DC: Author.

Council for Accreditation for Counseling and Related Education Programs. (1982). *Accreditation procedures manual for counseling and related educational programs*. Gainesville, FL: Author.

Council for Accreditation for Counseling and Related Educational Programs. (1987). *Accreditation procedures manual for counseling and related educational programs*. Alexandria, VA: Author.

Council for Accreditation for Counseling and Related Educational Programs. (1988). *Accreditation procedures manual and application*. Alexandria, VA: Author.

Stripling, R.O., & Dugan, W.E. (1961). The cooperative study of counselor education standards. *Counselor Education and Supervision, 0,* 34–35.

CHAPTER 5

A View From the Profession: What We Think of Where We Are

Donald C. Waterstreet

The decade of the eighties has produced major advances in credentialing, accreditation, certification, and licensure/registration in the entire field of counseling. With many efforts firmly entrenched, such as CACREP and NBCC, and with many new entities being developed, the time seemed opportune to review the current status of credentialing from the perspective of ACES members. To determine the progress made and the views of counselor educators and counselors in the field, a survey was administered during the fall of 1989 at each regional ACES meeting. These data were collected as a part of the "Credentialing Revisited" theme of Michael Altekruse in preparation for his 1990–1991 ACES presidency. Because of this emphasis on credentialing, a committee representing the major constituencies of the counseling field had been appointed and charged to develop and implement a process to assess ACES members' overall view of credentialing.

The survey questionnaire developed and then distributed to those in attendance at the five regional ACES meetings held during the fall of 1989 was designed to assess ACES members' perceptions of various aspects of credentialing in counseling. Because members were asked to complete the questionnaire at the business session of each regional meeting, the committee received responses to the questionnaire from most members in attendance. The total number of respondents was 228. Some questions were not answered by all respondents; therefore the number of respondents for any given question ranged from 191 to 228. Unfortunately, the respondents were not separated by professional position or longevity in the field. In the absence of more detailed information, one has to assume that the data reflect the views of ACES members in general and of those who are primarily in academic positions.

The results of the survey are presented here in terms of both actual number of respondents and percentages. The data are reported for all regions combined. The data were collected in a modified five-point Likert format, but for reporting purposes the data have been collapsed to represent polar opinions on each item.

In the survey, questions were asked to determine the perceived necessity of each form of credentialing. Each form of credentialing was first defined to provide a common reference point for all respondents. The general directions asked the respondent to provide his or her opinion regarding the need for each form of credentialing. A presentation of the data with a summary comment regarding the general trend for each data item follows.

Registration and Licensure

Registration was defined as "a process authorized by state legislation to regulate the title of the profession." Data regarding registration are contained in Table 1. As can be readily noted, 60% of the respondents tended to view registration as essential, whereas 23% viewed it as unnecessary. Because over half viewed registration as highly important, it would seem that this form of credential is viewed as important to the profession.

Licensure was identified as "a process authorized by state legislation to regulate the practice and title of a profession." Licensure data are also contained in Table 1. Respondents provided strong support for licensure, as will be noted through the 86% who strongly believed licensure to be essential. By contrast, only 5% considered licensure to be unnecessary as a credentialing activity. It is presumed that the strong support for licensure is at least partly driven by interest in third-party payment and the assumption that licensure will further the movement toward health insurance payment for services.

Table 1
Views on Registration and Licensure

	Unnecessary		Undecided		Essential	
	(f)	(%)	(f)	(%)	(f)	(%)
Registration	51	23	35	16	129	60
Licensure	13	5	15	6	198	87

Certification

Certification was described as "a process of recognizing the competence of practitioners of a profession by officially authorizing them to use the title adopted by the profession." Certification can be awarded by voluntary association, agencies, or governmental bodies.

The data describing the perceptions of various forms of certification are contained in Table 2. It should be noted that for agency certification the example of Certified Alcohol Counselor was provided. Also, for governmental certification state departments of education were identified as representative forms. Support for these areas of credentialing was fairly balanced across the various types. The possible exception was in the career area where a slightly larger number viewed this form as unnecessary and a slightly smaller number viewed it as essential. Possibly the reason for this lesser support is the fact that counselor educators are more involved in the broader scope of training. It is interesting to note that certification is viewed as less important than licensure. Explanations for this difference may lie in the current attention licensure is receiving or in the view of counselor educators that licensure is a bench mark effort for the development of a profession.

Table 2
Views on Certification

Type	Unnecessary		Undecided		Essential	
	(f)	(%)	(f)	(%)	(f)	(%)
NCC	56	24	26	11	146	64
CCMHC	76	36	31	14	89	50
Career	89	40	48	22	85	38
Supervision	66	29	39	17	121	53
Agency	68	30	44	20	112	50
Governmental	80	36	27	12	115	52

Accreditation

Accreditation was regarded as "a process whereby an association or agency grants public recognition to a school, institute, college, university, or specialized program of study that has met certain established qualifications or standards as determined through initial and periodic evaluations."

The data contained in Table 3 summarize the respondents' reactions to the issue of accreditation. Most notable is the fact that CACREP received very strong support: 85% perceived this form of accreditation to be essential. In many ways this is predictable because counselor educators were the primary respondents. Also, this response may indicate that the program standards set forth by CACREP are perceived as very important to quality training. The only other category of accreditation receiving very strong support was program approval, such as that provided by state departments of education. The latter is predictable because most, if not all, counselor education programs train public school counselors. The lack of strong support for the other forms of accreditation may simply be because counselor educators in general do not see themselves as directly involved in these forms.

Table 3
Views on Accreditation

Type	Unnecessary		Undecided		Essential	
	(f)	(%)	(f)	(%)	(f)	(%)
CACREP	16	6	19	8	150	85
CORE	58	30	40	21	53	28
NCATE	49	23	33	15	86	40
Regional	79	39	27	13	97	48
Program						
approval	40	18	19	9	155	73

Summary

ACES members who completed the questionnaire indicated support for most areas addressed in the questionnaire, with the possible exception of the career certification. The show of support for the credentialing currently in place was impressive; however, the data did not provide specific reasons for the members' responses to particular items on the questionnaire. Even when the data indicated overwhelming support, e.g., for licensure and CACREP, further conclusions could not be drawn because the initial questionnaire did not elicit reasons for the support or nonsupport. It would be interesting to know not only the basis for respondents' perceptions but also their views on credentialing for various subgroups within the field of counseling. For example, NCC certification for school counselors is currently under consideration. It would be interesting to know the reactions of ACES members to this issue. And what were the reasons for the split endorsement/nonendorsement of CCMHC certification? A follow-up questionnaire has been planned by the Credentialing Revisited Committee to elicit specific information.

Also interesting might be to solicit evaluations by counselor educators based on longevity in the field or primary training interest. Finally, the questionnaire could be used with other members of the counseling community, for example, with mental health counselors, school counselors, and student development administrators or counselors.

Recommendations

Based on this initial effort to evaluate perceptions of the various aspects of credentialing in counseling, the Credentialing Revisited Committee has recommended:

1. that a follow-up questionnaire be developed to solicit specific responses from ACES members regarding the various forms of credentialing.
2. that programs on credentialing be conducted at each regional meeting to solicit the reactions of ACES members to particular forms of credentialing.
3. that an effort be made to establish a linkage between ACES and the AACD Task Force on Credentialing to insure that ACES remains actively involved in the credentialing efforts.
4. that ACES, through the Credentialing Revisited Committee, explore the possibility of collaborative activity between NBCC, CACREP, and certification divisions of state departments to develop a model for states for use in school counselor certification; and that possibly a model be developed that would alleviate some or most of the duplication of efforts that currently are used in most school counseling certifications.

Most important to note from this initial questionnaire is that ACES members were very interested in credentialing and supported the need for counselor training institutions and counselors to be involved in various credentialing activities.

CHAPTER 6

Concerns About Accreditation and Credentialing: A Personal View

Kenneth B. Hoyt

Introduction

The National Association of Guidance Supervisors and Counselor Trainers (NAGSCT) launched "The Cooperative Study of Counselor Education Standards" in 1960—the same year in which its name was changed to Association for Counselor Education and Supervision. The stated planned outcome of this study, undertaken by a committee co-chaired by Willis Dugan and Robert O. Stripling, was "publication of a comprehensive report for use by professional personnel and counselor education institutions for the upgrading of counselor preparation programs" (Stripling & Dugan, 1961). At the ACES 1964 national convention in San Francisco, a spirited debate took place between those favoring and those opposing adoption of the standards developed and presented by the committee. In the end, a majority of those ACES members attending the ACES business meeting voted to approve the committee recommendations on steps necessary to implement the counselor education standards report (Miller, 1964). Even though the standards were officially adopted as "tentative" for a 3-year period, however, it was voted that the word *tentative* should not be used in the title of the report to be distributed to others (Hoyt, 1964). Instead, the printed version of the report carried the title "Standards for Counselor Education in the Preparation of Secondary School Counselors."

At that point, I ceased fighting this ACES effort to move toward accreditation of counselor education programs. So did almost all others on the "losing" side. The monograph in which this article appears stands as convincing evidence that ACES has made great progress since 1964 both in its efforts to formulate a means of accrediting counselor education institutions and in promoting various forms of credentialing for professional counselors. This does not mean that the objections raised during the 1960–1964 period no longer exist. They certainly do. Neither does it mean that such objections are *necessarily* lacking in logic or validity.

This chapter is an attempt to respond to a request to identify continuing objections that exist both to accreditation of counselor education programs and to credentialing of professional counselors. In attempting to meet this request, I have no desire to—nor do I intend to—restart the professional "wars" between opponents and proponents of accreditation and credentialing. The proponents have already won that war. Rather, this is merely an attempt to specify and explain basic concerns/objections regarding these matters that I have held since 1960. *I am simply doing what I was asked to do.*

Background

My interest in "accreditation" first became one of my professional priorities in 1961. At that time, I had concluded, after studying U.S. Department of Labor occupational projections, that the need for many high school graduates to pursue career goals demanding postsecondary sub-baccalaureate degree training was growing and that helping youth make such decisions must become a major component of the school counselor role and function. The primary kinds of postsecondary educational institutions providing such training at that time were proprietary trade/technical/business schools. When I started studying such schools, I discovered that some were accredited but others were not. Although I *assumed* that "accredited" institutions must be better than "nonaccredited" institutions, I could find no way of validating that assumption. Accredited schools simply claimed they were "good," whereas nonaccredited schools contended accreditation didn't matter.

In an effort to become more knowledgeable about how to help high school students make decisions regarding attendance at postsecondary sub-baccalaureate degree institutions, I listened to a great number of tape-recorded counseling interviews between school counselors and students considering such decisions. I was much impressed by the fact that the question "Is this institution accredited?" required only a few seconds to answer with a "Yes" or "No" reply. Almost all the rest of the interview centered around attempts to answer the question "What's likely to happen to ME if I enroll in this school?" The student's basic question was not "Is this a good school?" but rather "Is this a good school for ME?"

This was a major conceptual breakthrough for me. At that point, I made a decision to develop an alternative to accreditation through concentrating a major research effort aimed at helping youth answer the "Is this a good school for ME?" question. I wanted a system useful to counselors and students during the 49+ minutes of the counseling interview that remained after using 30 seconds to answer the "Is this school accredited?" question. This led to initiation of the Specialty Oriented Student (SOS) Research Program. The SOS Research Program aimed to (1) identify the most common "Is this a good school for ME?" questions high school students asked their counselors, (2) secure answers to those questions from present and former students in specific specialty institutions, and (3) report data back to counselors and students in the form of SOS Counselor Notebooks in which data collected from students in each specific training program in each participating SOS institution were reported as answers to questions being asked by high school students. My initial dream was to establish and operate a nationwide system that would, in effect, replace existing accreditation agencies for proprietary trade/technical/business schools.

The Next Step: Studying the Nature of Accreditation

In an attempt to emphasize the need for the SOS Research Program, I spent some time trying, in effect, to make the case against traditional accreditation procedures. The prime arguments I used included the following:

1. Accrediting bodies are typically initiated by a few institutions that are convinced that (a) their programs are of superior quality and (b) other institutions could improve their quality by changing in ways that will make them more similar to the few institutions that initiated the particular accrediting effort. There is typically no clear research base demonstrating the claimed superiority of those few institutions responsible for initiating an accreditation effort.
2. The prime measures used by accrediting bodies appear to concentrate much more on *program characteristics* (e.g., faculty/student ratio, percentage of faculty with advanced degrees, number of books in the library) than on *program outcomes* (e.g., placement rates, occupational successes of graduates, research efforts of faculty members).
3. There appear to be few, if any, researched relationships between criteria used by accrediting associations and the demonstrated successes of institutions seeking accreditation in meeting institutional program goals and objectives. Unless the applicant institution is similar to currently accredited institutions in a wide variety of ways, there is no way it can be accredited—no matter how well it meets its stated program goals and objectives.
4. The apparent intended goal of accrediting bodies is to make all "accredited" institutions appear "equally good" and all "nonaccredited" institutions appear "equally bad." Accredited institutions are simply listed by name, whereas all other institutions are ignored.

There is no way that the relative worth of accredited institutions is reported and/or can be determined by prospective students.

NOTE: Because I was formulating these observations during the period of time in which the ACES "standards committee" was actively seeking to develop "standards" for counselor education, it should not be difficult to understand why I was among those who voiced objections during the 1960–1964 period to this ACES project.

The SOS Research Program was formally established in 1962 at the University of Iowa. Just prior to its establishment, Virgil Hancher, then University of Iowa president, requested that I try to learn more about accreditation by visiting with William Seldon, then executive director of the National Commission on Accrediting (NCA) in Washington, DC. (I interpreted President Hancher's request to mean that, although he had no desire to restrict my expression of thoughts regarding accreditation, he felt I was probably wrong and would change my mind once I understood it better. I will forever be grateful to President Hancher for the way he handled this.) I was fascinated to learn that NCA's prime mission was to, in effect, "accredit" accrediting bodies. I spent several days visiting with Dr. Seldon and his staff members in their offices. Among the major things I learned, the following were most significant and meaningful to me:

1. The NCA (predecessor to COPA) was established and controlled primarily by university presidents. Its major purpose was to limit the number of accrediting bodies to the bare minimum necessary to ensure quality. (It appears that goal continues today as a COPA priority.)
2. NCA was dedicated to approving only those accrediting bodies whose criteria for accreditation appeared to consist of reasonable goals toward which higher education institutions should aspire, e.g., they tended *not* to approve accrediting bodies devised by various professional specialties that demanded huge expenditures of new funds for those universities seeking accreditation in that specialty.
3. Overall institutional accreditation was controlled primarily by regional accrediting bodies. NCA concerned itself primarily with accrediting bodies representing specialized disciplines within colleges and/or universities. It wanted to make sure that the "institutional self-improvement" aspects of a particular accrediting body would not place unreasonable financial requirements on the college/university.
4. The accreditation movement in general (including NCA) has a primary concern for identifying and insisting on *minimal* standards that all accredited institutions must meet, *not* on identifying differences among accredited institutions in a given specialty. An

inherent part of the nature of the accreditation process is to mask differences that exist among accredited institutions and instead to place all institutions in one of two broad categories—either accredited or nonaccredited.

Based on what NCA personnel taught me and the additional references they provided for me to study, I abandoned my original goal of replacing accreditation of proprietary trade/technical/business schools with the SOS Research Program. Instead, I adopted a position of viewing accreditation as a *necessary* but not a *sufficient* device for use in judging the worth of an institution. That continues to be my position today.

My support of accreditation was clearly stated in the initial policy statement announcing establishment of the Specialty Oriented Student Research Program:

> Accreditation as a concept in American education has consisted of decisions and judgments institutions and institutional members make regarding one another. Properly conducted, it is a valuable means of institutional self-improvement, of protecting the public from unsound, unfair, and dangerous practices, and of assuring the potential student of quality education. It allows those possessing the highest technical skills in particular educational areas to judge the degree to which quality educational opportunities in those areas are present in institutions applying for accreditation status. It is an indispensable part of American education. (Hoyt, 1962)

Background Leading to ACES Accreditation Initiatives

Before passage of the National Defense Education Act (NDEA) in 1958, considerable interest and activity had taken place with respect to counselor certification standards but not in accreditation of counselor education programs (Roeber, Smith, & Erickson, 1955). Between 1958 and 1961, Dugan (1961) reported that the number of counselor education programs grew from 175 to 475. I have a definite recollection of Harold McCully (deputy to Ralph Bedell, director, Counseling and Guidance Institutes Program, Title VB) stating that 90% of the persons listed as "director" of one of these 300 new programs had never been a counselor. Certainly, the need for institutional self-study and the kinds of facilitative assistance inherent in the accreditation process were clearly evident in these 300 new programs.

A second need leading to an accreditation emphasis was seen in operation of Title V–B—Counseling and Guidance Institutes—of NDEA. Title V–B not only provided generous subsidies to those counselor education programs awarded institutes but, in addition, provided generous student stipends as well. Applications poured in. The U.S. Office of Education

(USOE) had no standard way of judging which counselor education programs deserved to be awarded institutes and which should be rejected. As a result, the primary methodology used was for USOE to invite in a small number of counselor educators almost sure to be awarded institutes and ask them to make consensus judgments regarding all other applications. I was a member of that small group of "judges" and can attest to the fact that we often wished we had some standards for use in evaluating proposals. Two other judges were Robert Stripling (University of Florida) and Willis Dugan (University of Minnesota).

During the 1960–1964 period when the ACES standards committee was hard at work developing the standards and recommendations approved at the 1964 ACES convention, I can recall no arguments regarding the *need* for standards. However, two major arguments were raised regarding the *contents* of the proposed standards.

The first major argument centered around a recommendation for increasing the length of school counselor education programs from the master's degree level to 2 full years of graduate study. This recommendation obviously provided advantages to those counselor education institutions offering doctoral and/or specialist degrees in counseling and guidance—and handicapped smaller institutions where the master's degree was the highest awarded. If implemented, it had a clear practical advantage of greatly reducing the number of counselor education institutions eligible for NDEA Title V-B funding. Further, if counselors were required to pursue 2 full years of graduate study, we would be in a much better position to claim the counselor as a unique professional specialist—and thus as one for whom licensure would be appropriate (McCully, 1961).

In spite of the fact that I served as chair of a counselor education program in a doctoral granting university, I objected to this proposed standard on three grounds: (a) graduates from our 1-year master's degree program in school guidance/counseling were experiencing great success in finding and holding school counselor positions; (b) to insist on 2 years of graduate study for school counselors while other educators in K-12 school systems with whom they must work have no more than a master's degree held clear potential for creating possible conflicts; and (c) there was no experimental evidence of any kind justifying the need for 2 years—as opposed to 1 year—of graduate education for prospective school counselors.

The second major argument centered around what many considered to be an unduly great emphasis on the counseling practicum in the total counselor education program. Both the facilities and the faculty/student ratios called for in the standards were ones many existing counselor education institutions would have great difficulty in meeting. Further, once again, this expensive recommendation was made in the complete absence of any body of research data justifying its need. This was my prime objection.

Both arguments—and many others—were settled by the historic 1964 vote at the ACES San Francisco convention. From that moment on, some form of accreditation of counselor education institutions was inevitable. It was just a question of time.

Current Concerns Regarding Counselor Education Program Accreditation

Four kinds of major concerns continue to exist for me. The first is my continuing concern for the use of standards that have, so far as I can tell, no evidence of validity behind them. Examples (taken from the 1988 CACREP standards) call for such things as (1) a mininum of three full-time faculty members plus two additional faculty members in each specialty program area under CACREP review; (2) a requirement that an entry-level program be 2 years in length; (3) a requirement for a minimum of 100 clock hours in practicum of which 40 hours should be in direct service work; (4) a requirement for 600 clock hours of internship; (5) a requirement for the ratio of FTE students to FTE faculty to be no greater than 10:1; and (6) a requirement to provide one paid graduate assistantship for every 30 FTE students. As counselor educators, we are *supposed* to possess at least *some* knowledge regarding both measurement and research—and some commitment to using that knowledge. The fact that it is common practice in accrediting bodies to use arbitrary numbers as standards does not mean that the use of such practices by the counselor education movement is justified. The use of numbers does not make a subjective process an objective one. We know better—and we *should* do better.

My second concern has to do with the commonly accepted practices of accrediting bodies that make all accredited institutions look alike, look like the "cowboy with the white hat." This is not helpful to the prospective counselor education student who is trying to decide which of the accredited counselor education institutions would be best for him or her. Further, this practice of purposely masking differences that exist among accredited institutions is almost sure to promote a "let the minimum become the maximum" approach to determining the breadth and depth of the counselor education program. In an attempt to avoid this, if the *minimum* number of clock hours required for the entry level practicum is, say, 100, I would like to see published the *actual* number of hours required at each accredited counselor education institution. To adopt such a practice would, it seems to me, bring an additional welcome breath of intellectual honesty to the already highly regarded accreditation movement.

My third concern centers around the ways in which accrediting bodies, in their efforts to impose specific standards and procedures on programs applying for accreditation, run the risk of discouraging innovative and creative approaches to counselor education. Currently, the need for professional counselors in industrial, adult education, and community services agencies is increasing at a rapid rate. Who among us now claims to know exactly how best to prepare counselors to serve displaced workers? Retired persons? Single heads of household? Much evidence is being reported on how the values and behaviors of today's youth differ from those of previous generations. Are such differences to be ignored by counselor education programs as part of the price to be paid in order to meet accreditation standards? The need for new and creative approaches to counselor education has never been greater. It seems to me that uniform accreditation standards operating, in effect, so as to lower the probabilities that this need will be met should be discouraged.

My fourth concern centers around the need for prospective counselor education students (and others) to know much more than simply whether or not the counselor education program has been accredited. Once the prospective student has determined that a number of counselor education programs he or she is considering are "good" in that they are accredited, the question then becomes "Which of these institutions is the best one for me?" To answer this question, a variety of other kinds of data are needed. Examples include:

1. What kind(s) of counselors does the program claim to produce?
2. How many full-time and FTE students of each kind are currently enrolled?
3. How many graduates of each kind of counselor education program have been placed as counselors?
4. How do graduates of each kind of counselor education program evaluate the program?
5. What is the record of financial aid that has been made available to students in each kind of program? What is the current picture?
6. What are the institution's policies on racism and sexism?
7. What is the research and publication record of each professor in each kind of program?
8. What are the titles of theses and dissertations produced by graduates of each kind of program over the last 5 years?
9. What is the philosophical base for each kind of counselor education program?

I find it difficult to understand how counselor education institutions can, in good conscience, deny the need for producing and distributing these kinds of data needed for counseling prospective students. Granted, these data go far beyond what is traditionally meant by accreditation. That is why I continue to maintain a position that accreditation is a necessary but not a sufficient basis for use by a prospective counselor seeking to judge the worth of a particular counselor education institution.

Informal Thoughts on Credentialing

The title of this monograph concentrates on the word *credentialing* rather than the word *accreditation*. Thus, before concluding these observations, I feel a need to express a few personal thoughts on credentialing. My prime credentialing concerns over the years have centered mostly around the topic of state department of education certification of school counselors. Here, I have worked especially hard to defend a requirement that both a teaching certificate and successful K-12 teaching experience be prerequisites to school counselor certification (Hoyt, 1963). Other than this, I have devoted relatively little of my time, thoughts, or efforts to the topic of credentialing. My goal here is to explain my actions, not to attack the concept of credentialing. As with accreditation, there has already been far too much "water over the dam" to make it practical to object to the concept.

My relative lack of concern for the newer forms of credentialing stems primarily from the fact that my prime interests in counselor education have, over the years, centered mainly around the area of school counselor education programs. Since school counselors have, historically, been "certified" by state departments of education, I have considered such forms of credentialing as "licensure" and "registry" to be relatively unimportant with respect to my primary concerns.

When the National Certified Counselor (NCC) program was initially announced, I was interested in seeing how it was conceptualized and implemented. As soon as I discovered the generous grandfather clause provisions of the NCC group, I lost most of my interest. Whenever I see a counselor using the NCC title behind her or his name, I cannot help but wonder whether or not that person is a "grandfathered" NCC. As a result, the term *NCC* currently means very little to me.

In a logical sense, it is easy to understand why a national program of certification or licensure would be desirable for school counselors if they could use such certification or licensure as a means of moving from state to state as a certified counselor. Perhaps this has now occurred. I admit I have not studied the literature on this matter. However, I know of no specific actions yet taken by any state department of education to accept state licensure and/or a National Certified Counselor document as a substitute for its own counselor certification requirements. Until and unless this occurs, I see little advantage in school counselors seeking either licensure or NCC status unless they want to operate a private practice or community services in addition to working in a K-12 school district. In terms of my own students, it seems to me that the fact they have graduated from the counselor education program in which I work coupled with their official certification as a professional school counselor by the state department of education serve as clear evidence of their qualifications to begin working as a school counselor.

If licensure and/or NCC status are to be awarded to school counselors on top of their graduate degrees and state department of education certification, it seems to me such additional forms of attesting to the qualifications of counselors should be based primarily on behavioral indicators of success and not on how they score on a paper-and-pencil test constructed by those in charge of licensure and/or NCC programs. I particularly object to paper-and-pencil tests whose items are taken from the substantive content of the counselor education curriculum. My objection is that this will almost surely affect what professors of counselor education teach. As counselors, most of us know full well the dangers of a "teaching to the test" approach to education. It seems to me we have a professional obligation to avoid letting this become common practice in newer forms of counselor credentialing.

By behavioral indicators I am thinking, for example, in the case of a person requesting licensure and/or NCC status, that only currently employed counselors be eligible to apply. Such counselors would be asked to submit, for review by a panel of, say, three experts, such things as (1) complete case records for one or more clients, (2) several tape-recorded counseling interviews, (3) a description and written defense of the assessment procedures they use, (4) a description and written defense of the educational/ career information (if any) that they use, (5) a description and written defense of their use of community/referral resources, and (6) a series of several recommendations from a variety of sources, including clients. Granted, this would clearly be a subjective approach to credentialing. However, it might be better than current procedures, which, by arbitrarily assigning numbers to various requirements, are also subjective even if they do not appear to be. *Perhaps* this is what is happening in one or more states now. If so, I would be fully supportive of the effort.

A further advantage of a behavioral indicator approach to counselor licensure is the potential such an approach holds for combatting two potentially dangerous assumptions some supporters of licensure seem to be making. These assumptions are (1) that the counselor works primarily alone in helping clients and (2) that the counseling relationship is the most valuable tool available to the counselor. These kinds of assumptions *may* be appropriate and necessary for the entrepreneurial counselor in private practice. However, in terms of professional school counselors, they are potentially dangerous to the extent they negate or downplay two vital assumptions regarding school counselor role and function; namely (1) that the counselor is a member of a *team* of persons dedicated to meeting the developmental personal/social/educational/career needs of persons and (2) that the counseling relationship may not be the most important or effective way of providing the kinds of help some clients need.

Finally, in terms of credentialing issues, I find myself becoming increasingly interested in various forms of credentialing that can appropriately be made available to professional career development specialists. Many such specialists work in nonschool settings and with adults as well as with youth. Increasing numbers are in private practice. No valid reason exists, so far as I know, as to why these new kinds of career development specialists necessarily need to undergo a graduate-level program of counselor education. (After all, the prime reason counselor education became a graduate program was a USOE pronouncement in the late 1940s that school counselors should possess a valid teaching certificate and successful teaching experience.) Surely *some* form of credentialing could be constructed and used that would meet this need.

Concluding Remarks

This article has been written in response to a specific request for an expression of my personal concerns regarding credentialing and accreditation in counselor education. As I understand it, this request was made, in part, as an attempt on the part of the editor of this monograph to allow negative as well as positive points of view to be expressed. In part, this article was requested in order to clarify concerns that current leaders in counselor accreditation and licensure may choose to identify as barriers to be overcome.

I have tried to emphasize, at several points, the fact that I am not currently "fighting" either accreditation or credentialing. I never have fought either *concept*. My objections over the years have dealt primarily with the *means*, not the *ends*. Although the reservations expressed in this article continue to be important to me, I recognize and acknowledge that they have little practical meaning in today's counselor education movement. Perhaps that is all the more reason why it is important that they be expressed if only for their potential historical value. I very much appreciate the opportunity afforded me for doing so.

References

Dugan, W. (1961). Critical concerns of counselor education. *Counselor Education and Supervision, 0*(0), 5–11.

Hoyt, K. (1964). A vote against honesty [Editorial]. *Counselor Education and Supervision, 3*(2), 114.

Hoyt, K. (1963). Should school counselors have taught? A research proposal. *Counselor Education and Supervision, 2*(3), 126–129.

Hoyt, K. (1962). *An introduction to the Specialty Oriented Student Research Program.* Iowa City: University of Iowa Press.

McCully, C.H. (1961). A rationale for counselor certification. *Counselor Education and Supervision*, *1*(1), 3–9.

Miller, L. (1964). The president's message. *Counselor Education and Supervision*, *3*(2), 112–113.

Roeber, E., Smith, G., & Erickson, C. (1955). *Organization and administration of guidance services* (Ch. 4, Selection criteria, training, and certification of guidance workers). New York: McGraw-Hill.

Stripling, R., & Dugan, W. (1961). The cooperative study of counselor education standards. *Counselor Education and Supervision*, *0*(0), 34–35.

CHAPTER 7

An Argument for Credentialing

Theodore P. Remley

Credentialing is a necessary step in the professionalization of counseling. If the current credentialing activities were not taking place, we would not be able to justify our claim that we are moving rapidly toward our ultimate goal of establishing counseling as a profession that is separate and distinct from other mental health or educational professions. Despite the disadvantages inherent in separating legitimate counselors from those who do not qualify, credentialing is a process that is vital to our success as a profession.

Negative Consequences

All of the reasonable arguments against credentialing must be acknowledged. We have to recognize that the price to be paid for the professionalization of counseling includes distasteful consequences of credentialing.

Some individuals will be excluded from recognition as counselors even though they have skills that are equivalent to or are even greater than those of credentialed individuals. Some people in our society may not have access to counseling services who otherwise might have been served because some capable counselors will not be eligible for credentials. It is essential that the counseling profession avoid practices that arbitrarily exclude qualified individuals. Efforts must be made to define acceptable parameters broadly when establishing credentials so that few qualified counselors are excluded.

Once standards are set, creativity and innovation often are stifled. Those who aspire to meet established standards are conservative and hesitant to deviate from practices or methods that are certain to be acceptable. Those who sit on boards that issue credentials must be sensitive to this tendency of applicants to conform and encourage—or even demand—creativity in meeting the standards that have been set.

We must admit that credentials are expensive. Counselors who become credentialed must pay fees, and often the costs are passed on to consumers of counseling services. However, if credentials do result in a higher quality of counseling services and consumers are assured they are dealing with properly educated and knowledgeable counselors, the extra costs can be justified.

All of the negative consequences of credentialing are outweighed by the fact that credentialing is an essential step in the establishment of counseling as a profession. Without credentialing in the forms of graduate program accreditation, private certification at the national level, and state regulation of professional practice, counseling would never have a chance of achieving the status of a recognized profession.

Benefits

Credentialing has benefited counselors in numerous ways. Counseling has moved closer to being recognized in society as a true profession. Credentials have helped counselors in their attempts to be recognized as equals to other mental health or educational professionals. In the process of establishing credentials, counselors have been forced to define the process of counseling and agree upon the essential characteristics of a professional counselor. Finally, the public is better protected from unqualified and harmful counselors due to credentialing.

Professionalization

Caplow (1966) has identified four steps that are necessary before a group achieves full professional status. Counseling has accomplished the first three: forming a professional association (AACD); changing names to reduce identification with the previous lower occupational status (from guidance to counseling); and promulgating a code of conduct (AACD Ethical Standards, 1988). The fourth and last step toward professionalization is prolonged political agitation, including credentialing. Clearly counseling is politically active through passing state legislation that regulates counseling, attempting to achieve third-party insurance reimbursement for services rendered, demanding privileged communication statutes, and establishing national private credentialing boards.

A profession must be able to identify its members specifically. Counselors can be identified through credentials such as counseling graduate degrees from accredited colleges and universities, accredited graduate programs designed specifically to prepare counselors, certificates issued by private national boards, and certificates or licenses granted by state governments or agencies.

Parity

Credentials have helped counselors in their efforts to achieve parity with other mental health and educational professionals. An important trait of professionals is that they are capable of independent practice without supervision. Most scholars who have attempted to explain the difference between professionals and nonprofessionals have concluded that professionals hold credentials that allow them to be easily identified and entitle them to practice autonomously (Hughes, 1965; Phillips, 1982; Scott, 1969; Toren, 1969).

Counseling credentials both distinguish counselors from other similar professionals in mental health and education and imply that counselors have equal status to other professionals.

Definition

The credentialing movement has enhanced counseling with an unexpected benefit. Before counseling credentials could be established, the counseling process and the term *counselor* had to be specifically defined.

Counselors have been forced to examine themselves carefully and reach agreement as to what it is they do and who they are. This self-reflection that has been demanded of counselors by the process of creating credentials has strengthened our identity substantially.

Public Protection

The general public does not have the knowledge necessary to determine whether a person who claims to be a counselor is competent. In addition, incompetent counselors can inflict substantial harm upon their clients.

Credentials awarded by those who know how to identify capable counselors help protect the public. Voluntary credentials give consumers of counseling services an indication that a counselor has met certain minimal standards. Compulsory credentials, such as licenses issued by states, ensure that only those who are qualified are allowed to offer counseling services to the public.

Conclusion

Despite the problems credentials create, the positive effects they have had upon the professionalization of counseling substantially outweigh the arguments against credentials. If counseling had not become so vigorously involved in creating credentials, the field would not be so close to reaching the important status of a true profession.

Those who are involved in creating credentials and board members who award credentials must acknowledge the problems inherent in the credentialing process. It is hoped that counselors will be able to include all who are qualified and avoid the negative practice of arbitrarily excluding capable practitioners.

References

American Association for Counseling and Development. (1988). *Ethical standards.* Alexandria, VA: Author.

Caplow, T. (1966). The sequence of professionalization. In H.M. Vollmer & D.L. Mills (Eds.), *Professionalization.* Englewood Cliffs, NJ: Prentice Hall.

Hughes, E.C. (1965). Professions. In K.S. Lynn (Ed.), *The professions in America.* Boston: Houghton Mifflin.

Phillips, B.N. (1982). Regulation and control in psychology. *American Psychologist, 37,* 919–26.

Scott, W.R. (1969). Professional employees in a bureaucratic structure: Social work. In A. Etzioni, *The semi-professions and their organization.* New York: The Free Press.

Toren, N. (1969). Semi-professionalism and social work: A theoretical perspective. In A. Etzioni, *The semi-professions and their organization.* New York: The Free Press.

APPENDICES

APPENDIX A

A Summary of Counselor Credentialing Legislation

Carol S. Vroman and John W. Bloom

December 1990©

During the months of November and December 1990 phone calls were placed to the offices of the regulatory boards governing the practice of professional counseling in 34 states. Information gleaned from these interviews is presented here in summary form.

1. Column 1 presents the state name and the year in which the legislation was passed, along with the dates of any known amendments to the original legislation. Information about the sunset provisions contained in the legislation was also gathered. Although there is concern about the 18 state statutes that call for a sunset review, there is also concern about the four state boards that have been established but have not yet credentialed their first counselor (particularly the Delaware and Massachusetts boards, which were created in 1987).
2. Column 2 details the name of the regulatory board and the composition of these boards. Boards range in size from 3 in Vermont to 13 in Maine. The larger boards tend to be composite boards, such as the Arizona Board of Behavioral Health Examiners, which credentials counselors, social workers, family and marriage therapists, and substance abuse workers. In Arizona, a five-member subcommittee of the board recommends candidates for certification to the board.
3. Column 3 gives the mailing address and phone number of each board.
4. Column 4 gives the name of the administrator in charge of the regulatory board or a contact person. Also included in this column is the number of board employees and their job titles. Note that the long-established California board, which has credentialed 15,000 Licensed Marriage, Family, and Child Counselors, has a staff of 31 while newer boards may be fortunate to have 1 part-time employee.
5. Column 5 gives the formal title of the primary counseling professional credentialed in each state and the best estimate of the number of professionals currently credentialed with that title. Twenty-six of the 34 titles

include the word *professional*. Twenty-seven state boards credential professional counselors in general practice, while Delaware, Florida, Maine, Massachusetts, Rhode Island, Vermont, and Washington credential mental health counselors. The Ohio and Maine boards credential both.

6. Column 6 delineates the terminology used to describe the practice of counseling. Frequently used terms are *counsel, appraise, consult,* and *refer*. More recent legislation tends to include diagnosis and treatment language. And, in spite of our profession's concern about being proactive, only the Washington statute appears to contain verbiage that reflects developing "human potential."

7. Column 7 is potentially the most open to misinterpretation. Board employees were asked whether they considered the legislation to be voluntary or mandatory and to regulate title or practice. Licensure bills are generally considered to be mandatory and to regulate both title and practice, whereas certification bills are generally considered voluntary statutes that regulate title only. However, this often is not the case when one reads the fine print of the statutes.

8. In column 8 we can see that 15 boards regulate at least one other profession in addition to professional counseling and that 5 boards credential associate or assistant counselors. One board (South Carolina) credentials Licensed Professional Counselor Supervisors. The Texas and Massachusetts boards have the ability to credential rehabilitation counselors but have yet to do so.

9. Column 9 reflects that 22 of the statutes have created a 2-year credential. The cost of being credentialed for the first 2 years can also be determined by looking at the application and credential fee. (Note: Some states also have an exam fee that must be considered.) Exclusive of the exam fee, the range of fees for the first 2 years is from $100 or less in eight states to more than $400 in two states. The Massachusetts and South Dakota boards have not determined a fee structure yet.

10. In column 10, the education requirement column, the master's degree is required by every state board. Some states specify the minimum number of hours acceptable in the master's degree.

11. The experience requirement outlined in column 11 ranges from 1 year to 4 years, with the median experience requirement being 2 years. Supervision requirements vary similarly.

12. Column 12 shows that the examination accepted most frequently is the National Counselor Examination administered by the National Board for Certified Counselors (NBCC). Several states accept either the NBCC exam or the exam of the National Academy of Certified Clinical Mental Health Counselors or the exam of the Commission on Rehabilitation Counselor Certification. The California and Texas boards have created their own exams.

13. Finally, column 13 details the continuing education requirement. Twenty-four states do require some continuing education each year in order to renew one's credential and that requirement varies from 10 to 25 hours. The Michigan and Massachusetts boards have no continuing education requirement.

Note: As of December 1990, 34 states have passed some form of counselor credentialing legislation whether it be licensure, certification, or registry. Wide variations exist among these statutes, and one needs to examine each piece of legislation and the board's rules before drawing conclusions about the exact meaning of the terminology used in this summary.

State/Year Enacted/Year Amended/ Sunset Provision	Board Name/ (Number Board Members)— Board Composition	Board Address and Phone	Board Administrator and Staff Positions	Number/Title of Credentialed Counselors	Legally Defined Counselor Functions
Alabama (1979)/ No amendments/ No sunset provision	Alabama Board of Examiners in Counseling/ (7) 3 private practitioners, 2 counselor educators, 2 public	P.O. Box 550397, Birmingham, AL 35255 (205) 934-0498	Walter Cox, Executive Secretary (part time), one administrative assistant, one computer operator	650 Licensed Professional Counselors	Counsel, appraise, consult, refer, research
Arizona (1988)/ Amended 1989/ Sunset 1999	Board of Behavioral Health Examiners/(11) 2 each discipline, 3 public	1645 W. Adams, Suite 100A, Phoenix, AZ 85007 (602) 542-1882	David Oake, Executive Director (full time), 3 clerical (part time)	36 Certified Counselors	Diagnose/treat mental/physical disorders, address personal, social, educational, vocational development, and adjustment issues
Arkansas (1979)/ Amended 1989/ No sunset provision	Board of Examiners in Counseling/ (8) 3 professionals, 3 counselor educators, 1 general public, 1 retired citizen	Southern Arkansas University, P.O. Box 1396, Magnolia, AR 71753 (501) 235-4057	Ann K. Thomas, Executive Director (part time), Nancy Williams, secretary (part time)	350 Licensed Professional Counselors	Counsel, appraise, consult, refer, research
California (1964)/ Amendments: no info available/ No sunset provision	Board of Behavioral Science Examiners/ (11) 2 LCSWs, 2 MFCCs, 1 educational psychologist, 6 public	1021 O St., Sacramento, CA 95814 (916) 445-4933	Kathleen Callanan, Executive Officer, staff of 30	15,000 Licensed Marriage, Family, and Child Counselors	Apply psychotherapeutic techniques, address psychosexual and psychosocial aspects of relationships

*NBCC = National Board for Certified Counselors
NACCMHC = National Academy of Certified Clinical Mental Health Counselors
CRCC = Commission on Rehabilitation Counselor Certification
NCCC = National Certified Career Counselor (an NBCC specialty designation)

Mandatory or Voluntary- Regulation of Title or Practice	Other Credentials Regulated by Same Statute	Term of Credential— Credentialing Fees	Minimum Education Requirement	Experience Requirement	Examination Require- ment*	Continuing Education Requirement
Mandatory title and practice	None	2 year credential— $100 license $ 75 application $ 75 exam $100 renewal	Graduate degree, which includes 30 semester hours	3 years supervised experience, with 2 years being postmaster's	NBCC, oral and/or situational	20 hours per year in pre-approved programs
Voluntary title	Social work, marriage and family therapy, substance abuse	2-year credential— $125 initial $100 exam $100 renewal	Master's degree	2 years postmaster's experience, including 1 year under supervision	NBCC, CRC, or NACCMHC	20 hours per year
Mandatory title and practice	48 licensed associate counselors	2-year credential— $ 50 application $100 license $ 80 exam $150 renewal	Graduate degree with minimum of 48 semester hours	3 years supervised full-time experience, with 2 years being postmaster's	NBCC, oral and/or situational test optional	12 hours per year
Mandatory title and practice	Clinical social worker, educational psychologist	2-year credential— $300 application $150 renewal	2-year master's degree (48 hours)	2 years (3,000 hours) experience, with 1 hour of direct supervision for each week	Written state prepared exam and oral exam	None

State/Year Enacted/Year Amended/ Sunset Provision	Board Name/ (Number Board Members)— Board Composition	Board Address and Phone	Board Administrator and Staff Positions	Number/Title of Credentialed Counselors	Legally Defined Counselor Functions
Colorado (1988)/ No amendments/ Sunset 6/30/92	Board of Licensed Professional Counselor Examiners/ (7) 5 LPCs, 2 public	1560 Broadway, Suite 1340, Denver, CO 80202 (303) 894-7766	Karen Frazzini, Program Administrator, 1 secretary and 1 administrative assistant (all part time)	240 Licensed Professional Counselors	Treat, assess, consult, refer, conduct psychotherapy
Delaware (1987)/ Seeking amendments 1990–91/ Sunset—yes	Board of Professional Counselors/ (8) 5 LPCs, 3 public	P.O. Box 1401, Margaret O'Neill Bldg., Dover, DE 19903 (302) 739-4522	Vicki Hall, Administrative Assistant	0 Licensed Professional Counselors of Mental Health	Counsel, consult, refer, research
Florida (1981)/ Amended 1987/ Sunset 1999	Board of Clinical Social Workers, Marriage and Family Therapists, and Mental Health Counselors/ (9) 2 each discipline, 3 public	Florida Department of Professional Regulation, 1940 N. Monroe St., Tallahassee, FL 32399-0753 (904) 487-2520	Henry Dover, Executive Director, 1 application clerk, 1 discipline tracker, 1 manager, 1 continuing education clerk (all part time)	2,260 Licensed Mental Health Counselors	Counsel, assess, diagnosis and treat, describe, prevent, treat undesirable behaviors, client advocacy, crisis intervention, hypnotherapy
Georgia (1984)/ Amended 1990/ Sunset 1996	Composite Board of Professional Counselors, Social Workers, and Marriage and Family Therapists/ (10) 3 each discipline, 1 public	166 Pryor St., SW, Atlanta, GA 30303 (404) 656-3989	Lori Gold, Executive Director, Lillian Norton, Application Specialist, secretary (part time)	940 Licensed Professional Counselors	Assist, identify, consult, refer, research, assess, make vocational plan
Idaho (1982)/ No amendments/ Sunset 1991	Idaho State Counselor Licensing Board/ 4, all LPCs	Bureau of Occupational Licensure, 2417 Bank Dr., Room 312, Boise, ID 83705-2598 (208) 334-3233	Duane Higer, Executive Director (part time) Sherlene Cowley, Secretary to the Board (part time)	255 Licensed Professional Counselors	Not defined in law, but LPC must adhere to AACD Code of Ethics, which defines practice of counseling

Mandatory or Voluntary-Regulation of Title or Practice	Other Credentials Regulated by Same Statute	Term of Credential—Credentialing Fees	Minimum Education Requirement	Experience Requirement	Examination Require-ment*	Continuing Education Requirement
Voluntary title	Psychology, clinical social work, marriage and family therapy	1-year credential—$210 initial $230 renewal	Master's degree or doctorate	2 years postmaster's practice or 1 year postdoctoral practice under board approved supervision	NBCC	None
Voluntary title	None	2-year credential—fees not yet established	Graduate degree/must have NBCC or NACCMHC credential for state licensure	3 years full time/under supervision; 2 years must be postmaster's	Written, oral and/or situational; will accept NBCC	20 hours per year
Mandatory title (will become practice in 1995)	Sex therapy, hypnosis, clinical social work, marriage and family therapy	2-year credential—$250 exam $150 license $ 30 exam review $ 50 renewal	Master's degree, 60 semester hours or 90 quarter hours	3 years experience, 2 years must be supervised postmaster's	NACCMHC	15 hours per year
Mandatory title	Social work and marriage and family therapy	2-year credential—$100 application $ 50 exam $100 renewal $150 late renewal	Master's degree or higher	4 years postmaster's, with 1 year supervised experience	NBCC, oral and/or experiential	17½ hours per year
Voluntary title	None	1-year credential—$75 license $75 application $50 exam $60 renewal	Graduate degree, 60 semester hours	1,000 hours supervision by an LPC	NBCC	None

State/Year Enacted/Year Amended/ Sunset Provision	Board Name/ (Number Board Members)— Board Composition	Board Address and Phone	Board Administrator and Staff Positions	Number/Title of Credentialed Counselors	Legally Defined Counselor Functions
Kansas (1987)/ Amended 1989/ Sunset—1992	Behavioral Sciences Regulatory Board/ (7) 2 psychologists, 2 social workers, 3 public	Landon Office Bldg., Rm 855-S, 900 Jackson, Topeka, KS 66612-1220 (913) 296-3240	Mary Ann Gabel, Executive Director, 3 clerical (full time)	256 Registered Professional Counselors	Counsel, assess, consult, refer
Louisiana (1987)/ Amended 1988, 1989/ Sunset 1991	Licensed Professional Counselors Board of Examiners/ (7) 3 LPCs, 3 counselor educators, 1 public	4664 Jamestown Ave., Suite 125, Baton Rouge, LA 70808-3218 (504) 922-1499	Susan Mayeaux, Executive Director (full time), 1 clerical (part time)	1,561 Licensed Professional Counselors	Counsel, consult, refer, research
Maine (1989)/ Amended 1990/ Sunset—yes	Board of Counseling Professionals/ (13) 2 LPCs, 2 LCMHCs, 2 LM&FTs, 2 LPastoralCs, 1 faculty, 3 public, 1 ex officio	State House Station 35, Augusta, ME 04333 (207) 582-8723	Pat Beaudoin, Secretary to the Board	0 Licensed Professional Counselors	Counsel, assess, consult, refer
Maryland (1985)/ No amendments/ Sunset 7/1/94	Board of Examiners of Professional Counselors/ (6) 1 public counselor, 2 at large, 1 consumer, 1 counselor educator, 1 private counselor	Metro Executive Center, 3rd Fl., 4201 Patterson Ave., Baltimore, MD 21215-2299 (301) 764-4732	Aileen Taylor, Administrator (part time), 1 secretary (full time)	1,093 Certified Professional Counselors	Assist, test, appraise, refer, define goals, plan actions, make decisions
Massachusetts (1987)/ Amended 1989/ No sunset	Board of Allied Mental Health and Human Service Professionals/ (7) combination	100 Cambridge St., 15th Fl., Boston, MA 02202 (617) 338-1053	Terri Theaux, no staff yet.	0 Licensed Mental Health Counselors (seeking to add the word *Clinical*)	Counsel, treat, plan, prevent, refer

Mandatory or Voluntary-Regulation of Title or Practice	Other Credentials Regulated by Same Statute	Term of Credential—Credentialing Fees	Minimum Education Requirement	Experience Requirement	Examination Require-ment*	Continuing Education Requirement
Voluntary title	Psychology social work	2-year credential—$100 application $100 exam $100 renewal	60 semester hours as part of graduate degree	3 years postmaster's supervised	NBCC	25 hours per year
Mandatory title and practice	None	2-year credential—$200 application $100 exam $100 renewal	Graduate degree with 48 semester hours	2 years postmaster's experience (3,000 hours)	NBCC or oral	12½ hours per year
Mandatory title and practice	Clinical mental health counselors, marriage and family therapists, pastoral counselors	2-year credential—fees not established	Master's degree in counseling	2 years postmaster's experience plus 2,000 hours supervised clinical experience	Not determined	Yes—has to be defined
Voluntary title	Provisions for counseling specialties, career development, marriage and family, school, pastoral, and substance abuse (none used currently)	2-year credential—$50 application $50 certification $75 exam $60 reexam $50 renewal	Master's degree or doctorate with 60 graduate hours	3 years supervised experience, 2 years must be postmaster's	NBCC meets requirements for grand-parenting, not sure which exam will be used thereafter	20 hours per year proposed
Voluntary title	Marriage and family therapist, rehabilitation counselor, educational psychologist	Term of credential and fees not yet determined	Master's degree	2 years postmaster's; 100 hours supervision including 50 hours direct contact	Written or oral—accepting NACCMHC	Not stipulated

State/Year Enacted/Year Amended/ Sunset Provision	Board Name/ (Number Board Members)— Board Composition	Board Address and Phone	Board Administrator and Staff Positions	Number/Title of Credentialed Counselors	Legally Defined Counselor Functions
Michigan (1989)/ Amended 1990/ No sunset	Michigan Board of Counseling/ (9) 6 LPCs, 2 public, 1 mental health professional	P.O. Box 30018, Lansing, MI 48909 (517) 373-1870	Doris Foley, Administrative Assistant, umbrella staff	1,150 Licensed Professional Counselors	Counsel, developmental evaluation, appraise, guide, psychoeducational consult, prevent, behavior mod
Mississippi (1985)/ No amendments/ No sunset	Board of Examiners for LPCs/ (5) 2 private practitioners, 2 counselor educators, 1 public counselor	P.O. Drawer 6239, Mississippi State, MS 39762-6239 (601) 325-8182	Cathy Crockett, Secretary to the Board	274 Licensed Professional Counselors	Counsel, research, refer, appraise, assess, understand, predict, influence behavior
Missouri (1985)/ Amended 1989 No sunset	Missouri Committee for Professional Counselors/ (6) 5 professionals, 1 public	P.O. Box 162, Jefferson City, MO 65102 (314) 751-0018 Ext. 200	Charlotte Ronan, Executive Director, 2 clerical, 1 investigator	971 Licensed Professional Counselors	Counsel, appraise, refer, consult, research, understand, influence behavior
Montana (1983)/ LPCs added to social work bill in 1985/ Sunset—yes	Board of Social Work and LPC Examiners/ (7) 3 LPCs, 3 social workers, 1 public	111 N. Jackson, Arcade Bldg., Helena, MT 59620 (406) 444-4285	Mary Hainlin, Administrative Assistant (part time)	262 Licensed Professional Counselors	Counsel, appraise, technical assistance, refer, understand inter- and intrapersonal problems, defining goals
Nebraska (1986)/ Amended 1988/ No sunset	Board of Examiners in Professional Counseling/ (4) 3 CPCs, 1 public	Bureau of Examining Boards, 301 Centennial Mall S, P.O. Box 95007, Lincoln, NE 68509-5007 (402) 471-2115	Kris Chiles, Associate Director, 1 board coordinator, 1 clerical (all part time)	300 Certified Professional Counselors	Appraise, refer, research, rehabilitation, consult, define goals, plan actions, change behaviors

Mandatory or Voluntary-Regulation of Title or Practice	Other Credentials Regulated by Same Statute	Term of Credential—Credentialing Fees	Minimum Education Requirement	Experience Requirement	Examination Require-ment*	Continuing Education Requirement
Mandatory title and practice	None	1-year initial credential—3-year renewal. $100 application $ 50 renewal	Master's degree	2 years postmaster's supervised counseling experience	Not specified	Not defined
Mandatory practice	None	1-year credential— $100 application $100 exam $ 60 renewal	Master's degree 60 semester hours	2 years of supervised experience, 1 year must be postmaster's	NBCC; oral and/or situational	None
Mandatory practice	Clinical social work	1-year credential— $100 application $150 exam $ 50 exam score endorsement $125 renewal	Master's degree, 30 semester hours if credentialed before 7/1/91, 45 hours after	2 years postmaster's supervised experience, 1 year for EdS or doctoral	NBCC	None
Voluntary title	Social work	1-year credential— $75 license $75 application $75 exam $75 renewal	Advanced degree, 90 quarter hours or 60 semester hours	2,000 hours supervision, 50% must be postmaster's	NBCC	20 hours per year
Voluntary title	None	2-year credential— $200 application $175 renewal	Master's degree	3 years full-time postmaster's	NBCC or equivalent	20 hours per year

State/Year Enacted/Year Amended/ Sunset Provision	Board Name/ (Number Board Members)— Board Composition	Board Address and Phone	Board Administrator and Staff Positions	Number/Title of Credentialed Counselors	Legally Defined Counselor Functions
North Carolina (1983)/ No amendments/ No sunset	Registered Practicing Counselors Examiners/ (7) 2 counselor educators, 2 public counselors, 1 private counselor, 2 public	Box 12023, Raleigh, NC 27605 (919) 737-2244	Don C. Locke, Executive Director (part time)	533 Registered Practicing Counselors	Counsel, appraise, consult, refer, research, define goals, plan actions
North Dakota (1989)/ No amendments/ No sunset	Board of Counselor Examiners/ (5) 2 practicing counselors, 1 counselor educator, 2 public	P.O. Box 385, Beulah, ND 58523 (701) 873-4956	Julie Salveson-Duffey, Administrative Assistant (part time)	11 Licensed Professional Counselors	Counsel
Ohio (1984)/ Amended twice/ No sunset	Counselor and Social Worker Board/ (11) 4 counselors, 4 social workers, 2 public, 1 unspecified	77 South High St., 16th Fl., Columbus, OH 43266 (614) 466-6463	Beth Farnsworth, Executive Secretary, 2 investigators, 1 secretary, 1 renewal coordinator, 1 applications coordinator, 1 receptionist	4,000 Licensed Professional Counselors	Counsel, appraise, consult, refer, diagnose, assist, assess, analyze, explore solutions
Oklahoma (1985)/ No amendments/ No sunset	Licensed Professional Counselor Committee/ (5) 3 LPCs, 1 public, 1 health department employee	1000 NE 10th St., Oklahoma City, OK 73152 (405) 271-6030	Mike Blazi, Administrator, 1 assistant	890 Licensed Professional Counselors	Counsel, consult, refer, define goals, plan actions
Oregon (1989)/ No amendments/ Sunset 1997	Board of Licensed Professional Counselors & Therapists/ (7) 3 LPCs, 2 M&F, 1 faculty, 1 public	796 Winter St. NE, Salem, OR 97310 (503) 378-5499	Carol Fleming, Board Administrator (full time)	200 Licensed Professional Counselors	Counsel, research, refer, consult, facilitate change, assist, define goals, plan actions

Mandatory or Voluntary- Regulation of Title or Practice	Other Credentials Regulated by Same Statute	Term of Credential— Credentialing Fees	Minimum Education Requirement	Experience Requirement	Examination Require- ment*	Continuing Education Requirement
Voluntary title	None	2-year credential— $75 application $75 exam $50 renewal	Master's degree	2 years postmaster's supervised experience	NBCC	20 hours per year
Mandatory title	Licensed associate counselor	2-year credential— $140 initial $ 60 exam $ 60 renewal	Master's degree	2 years of supervision by LPC as licensed associate (after July 91)	NBCC (will also accept NACCMHC, NCCC)	15 hours per year
Mandatory title and practice	1,500 LP clinical counselors, 95 registered counselor assistants, licensed social worker, licensed independent social worker	2-year credential— $ 60 LPC $ 75 LPCC $100 NBCC and NACCMHC exam $ 60 LPC renewal $ 75 LPCC renewal	Master's degree, 60 quarter hours, 40 semester hours	3 years supervised experience of which 2 years must be postmaster's	NBCC for LPC, NACCMHC for LPCC	15 hours per year
Voluntary title	Not defined	2-year initial credential— $145 application $ 90 license $ 90 exam $ 80 annual renewal	Master's degree, 45 semester hours	3 years postapplication supervised experience (3,000 hours)	NBCC	20 hours per year
Voluntary title	Marriage and family therapists	1-year credential— $65 application $65 license $50 exam $65 renewal	Graduate degree, 48 semester hours	3 years of full-time supervised experience or equivalent	Written exam—NBCC agreement under negotiation	20 hours per year

State/Year Enacted/Year Amended/ Sunset Provision	Board Name/ (Number Board Members)— Board Composition	Board Address and Phone	Board Administrator and Staff Positions	Number/Title of Credentialed Counselors	Legally Defined Counselor Functions
Rhode Island (1987)/ Amended 1987/ No sunset	Board MHC's and Marriage and Family Therapists/ (7) 2 public, 3 MHCs, 2 M&F	Division of Professional Regulation, 3 Capitol Hill, Cannon Bldg., Room 104, Providence, RI 02908-5097 (401) 277-2827	Peter Petrone, Administrative Officer (part time), 1 support staff	20 Certified Counselors in Mental Health	Counsel, refer, define goals, develop plans
South Carolina (1985)/ Amended 1987, 1988/ Sunset 1991 (6 years)	Board of Examiners in Counseling/ (8) 3 counselors, 3 marriage and family therapists, 2 at large	P.O. Box 7965, Columbia, SC 29202 (803) 734-1765	Executive Secretary (full time), 1 part time bookkeeper	750 Licensed Professional Counselors	Assist people through counseling and psychotherapeutic relationship, appraise, consult, refer
South Dakota (1990)/ No amendments No sunset	South Dakota Board of Counselor Examiners/ (5) 4 LPCs, 1 public	1101 Bridgeview, Pierre, SD 57501 (605) 224-7172	Mavis Booze, Secretary/ Treasurer to the Board	0 Licensed Professional Counselors	Counsel, define goals, plan actions, understand personal problems
Tennessee (1984)/ No amendments/ Sunset 7 years	Board of Certification for Professional Counselors and Marriage and Family Therapists/ (5) 2 CM&FTs, 2 CPCs, 1 public	283 Plus Park Blvd., Nashville, TN 37247-1010 (615) 367-6207	Elaine O'Connor, Administrator, 1 secretary (part time)	1,005 Certified Professional Counselors	Facilitate human growth and development through the life stages, educate, assess, consult, research
Texas (1981)/ Amended 1983, 1985, 1989/ Sunset Sept 1993	Board of Examiners of Professional Counselors/ (9) 4 counselors in private practice, 1 counselor educator, 4 public	1100 W. 49th St., Austin, TX 78756-3183 (512) 459-2900	Don Rettberg, Executive Secretary (full time), 1 education coordinator, 1 licensing and app tech, 1 board secretary, 1 receptionist, 2 continuing educ techs, 1 licensing supervisor	7,157 Licensed Professional Counselors	Counsel, guide, appraise, consult, refer, research, define goals, plan action, understand personal problems

Mandatory or Voluntary-Regulation of Title or Practice	Other Credentials Regulated by Same Statute	Term of Credential—Credentialing Fees	Minimum Education Requirement	Experience Requirement	Examination Require-ment*	Continuing Education Requirement
Voluntary title	40 marriage and family therapists	2-year credential—$350 application $200 renewal	Graduate degree, 60 semester or 90 quarter hours and must be certified by NACCMHC	2 years (2,000 hours) direct contact postmaster's; 100 hours postmaster's supervision	NACCMHC and/or oral	None
Voluntary title	29 licensed associate counselors, 192 licensed professional counselors, supervisors, marriage and family therapists	2-year credential—$ 75 application $150 license $ 60 exam $150 renewal	Master's degree, 30 semester hours	2 years postmaster's with 150 hours supervision	NBCC, oral and/or situational	20 hours per year
Voluntary title	None	Not yet established	Master's or doctoral degree, 48 semester hours	1,800 hours of supervised full-time experience, 50% must be postmaster's	Yes—not defined at present	Yes–not defined
Voluntary title	70 certified associate counselors, marriage and family therapists	1-year credential—$140 initial $ 45 renewal	60 semester hour master's degree	2 years subsequent to degree	Yes—not defined at present	10 hours per year
Voluntary title	Rehabilitation counselors, drug and alcohol and art therapy have petitioned	1-year credential—$30 application plus $3/month from date of issue to birth month $30 exam $30 renewal	Graduate degree, 45 semester hours	2 years or 2,000 hours supervised experience	Field exam or state-developed written exam	25 hours per year

State/Year Enacted/Year Amended/ Sunset Provision	Board Name/ (Number Board Members)— Board Composition	Board Address and Phone	Board Administrator and Staff Positions	Number/Title of Credentialed Counselors	Legally Defined Counselor Functions
Vermont (1988)/ No amendments/ Sunset—yes	CCMHC Advisory Board/ (3) 2 professionals, 1 public	Pavillion Office Bldg., Montpelier, VT 05602 (802) 828-2390	Diane LaFaille, Secretary	87 Certified Clinical Mental Health Counselors	Utilize psychotherapeutic techniques to promote optimal mental health, define goals, plan actions, consult, refer
Virginia (1975)/ Amended—yes/ No sunset	Board of Professional Counselors/ (9) 7 LPCs, 2 public	Department of Health Regulation Boards, 1601 Rolling Hills Dr., Richmond, VA 23229-5005 (804) 662-9912	Evelyn Brown, Executive Director (part time), one administrative assistant (full time)	1,226 Licensed Professional Counselors	Counsel, guide, appraise, consult, refer, understand personal problems, define goals, plan actions
Washington (1987)/ No amendments/ Sunset 1995	Mental Health Counselors' Advisory Committee/ (5) 4 professionals, 1 public	1300 SE Quince St., Olympia, WA 98504 (206) 586-8584	Barbara Hayes, Program Manager, 3 clerical	1,800 Certified Mental Health Counselors	Employ therapeutic techniques to achieve sensitivity and awareness of self and others, develop human potential
West Virginia (1986)/ No amendments/ Sunset 1992 (5 years)	Board of Examiners in Counseling/ (7) 2 public, 3 LPCs, 2 counselor educators	P.O. Box 6492, Charleston, WV 25362 (304) 345-3852	Charles Maine, Administrator, 1 secretary	891 Licensed Professional Counselors	Assess, supervise, refer, place, contribute to self understanding
Wyoming (1987)/ No amendments/ No sunset	Mental Health Professionals Licensure Board/ (6) 1 each discipline, 2 public	Barrett Bldg., 2301 Central Ave., Cheyenne, WY 82002 (307) 777-6529	Felicia Adkinson, Secretary (part time)	300 Licensed Professional Counselors	Acts/behaviors coming within the meaning established by national and professional organizations representing specializations

Mandatory or Voluntary-Regulation of Title or Practice	Other Credentials Regulated by Same Statute	Term of Credential—Credentialing Fees	Minimum Education Requirement	Experience Requirement	Examination Require-ment*	Continuing Education Requirement
Voluntary title	None	2-year credential— $ 60 application $100 exam $ 75 renewal	Master's degree	2 years postmaster's experience and a minimum of 100 hours of face-to-face supervision	NACCMHC	20 hours per year
Mandatory practice	None	1-year credential— $100 application $150 exam $ 75 renewal	Graduate study of 60 semester hours to include a graduate degree	2 years postgraduate supervised experience (4,000 hours) with 200 hours face-to-face supervision	NBCC and/or oral exam	None
Voluntary title	Social work, marriage and family therapy	2-year credential— $131 application $145 exam $ 73.50 renewal	Master's degree; 30 semester/45 quarter hours	2 years postmaster's supervised with 100 hours face-to-face supervision	NBCC or NACCMHC	None
Mandatory title and practice	None	2-year credential— $50 application $80 exam $25 renewal	Master's degree	2 years professional supervision of which 1 year must be postmaster's	NBCC or CRCC	20 hours per year
Voluntary, title	Social work, marriage and family therapy, addiction specialists	2-year credential— $60 application $50 license $50 exam $50 renewal	Master's degree or equivalent (45 credits)	3,000 hours postmaster's including 100 hours face-to-face supervision	NBCC, NACCMHC, CRCC	22.5 hours per year

Licensed Professional Counselors

Alabama	650
Arkansas	350
Colorado	240
Georgia	940
Idaho	255
Louisiana	1,561
Maine	0
Michigan	1,150
Mississippi	274
Missouri	971
Montana	262
North Dakota	11
Ohio	4,000
Oklahoma	890
Oregon	200
South Carolina	750
South Dakota	0
Texas	7,157
Virginia	1,226
West Virginia	891
Wyoming	300
Total	**22,078**

Certified Professional Counselors

Arizona	36
Maryland	1,093
Nebraska	300
Tennessee	1,005
Total	**2,430**

Registered Professional Counselors

Kansas	256
North Carolina	533
Total	**789**

Licensed Professional Counselor Supervisors

South Carolina	192

Licensed Rehabilitation Counselors

Massachusetts	0
Texas	0

Licensed/Certified Mental Health Counselors

Delaware	0
Florida	2,260
Maine	0
Massachusetts	0
Ohio	1,500
Rhode Island	20
Vermont	87
Washington	1,800
Total	**5,667**

Licensed Marriage, Family, And Child Counselors

California	15,000

Credentialed Associate Counselors

Arkansas	48
North Dakota	0
Ohio	95
South Carolina	29
Tennessee	70
Total	**242**

GRAND TOTAL
46,402 (12/14/90)

APPENDIX B

Professional Certifying Bodies

Academy of Certified Social Workers
7981 Eastern Avenue
Silver Spring, MD 20910

American Association of Marriage and
Family Therapists
1717 K Street N.W. #407
Washington, DC, N.W.
(202) 429-1825

American Association of State
Counseling Boards
P.O. Drawer GE
Mississippi State University
Mississippi State, MS 39762
(601) 325-3426

American Association of State
Psychology Boards
P.O. Box 4389
555 South Perry Street
Suite 112
Montgomery, AL 36103

American Association of Social Work
Boards
718 Arch Street
Philadelphia, PA 19106

American Occupational Therapy
Certification Board
1383 Piccard Drive
P.O. Box 1725
Rockville, MD 20850-4375

Certification Board for Music Therapists,
Inc.
1133 15th Street, N.W.
Suite 1000
Washington, DC 20005

Commission on Rehabilitation Counselor
Certification
1156 Shure Drive
Suite 350
Arlington Heights, IL 60004
(312) 394-2104

Council for the National Register of
Health Service Providers in
Psychology
1730 Rhode Island Avenue, N.W.
Suite 1200
Washington, DC 20036

International Association of Marriage and
Family Counselors
University of Colorado at Denver
1200 Larimer Street
Box 106
Denver, CO 80202
(303) 556-2563

National Academy of Certified Clinical
Mental Health Counselors
5999 Stevenson Avenue
Alexandria, VA 22304
(703) 461-6222

Source: Collison, B.B., & Garfield, N.J. (1990). *Careers in counseling and human development.* Alexandria, VA: American Association for Counseling and Development.

National Board of Certified Counselors
5999 Stevenson Avenue
Alexandria, VA 22304
(703) 461-6222

National Coalition of Art Therapy
  Assocation
505 Eleventh Street, S.E.
Washington, DC 20003
(202) 543-6864

National Council for the Accreditation of
  Teacher Education
1919 Pennsylvania Avenue, N.W.
Suite 202
Washington, DC 20006
(202) 466-7496

National Council for Therapeutic
  Recreation Certification
P.O. Box 16126
Alexandria, VA 22302

NASW Register of Clinical Social
  Workers
7981 Eastern Avenue
Silver Spring, MD 20910

APPENDIX C

Directory of Accredited Programs

ALABAMA

Counseling and Counseling Psychology
2014 Haley Center
Auburn University
Auburn University, AL 36849-5222
CCOAS, SC, SPC (1994)
☆CE:PhD/EdD (1991)

Counselor Education
Graves Hall
University of Alabama
P.O. Box 870231
Tuscaloosa, AL 35487-0231
☆CC, SC, SAC, CE:PhD/EdD (1991)

BRITISH COLUMBIA

Department of Counseling Psychology
University of British Columbia
5780 Toronto Road
Vancouver, B.C. CANADA V6T 1L2
☆CCOAS, SC, SPC (1991)

CALIFORNIA

Division of Administration and
  Counseling
CSU/Los Angeles
5151 State University Drive
Los Angeles, CA 90032
SC, SPC (1994)

Educational Psychology and Counseling
CSU/Northridge
1811 Nordhoff Street
Northridge, CA 91330
CCOAS, SC (1993)

Department of Counseling
CSU/Sacramento
6000 J Street
Sacramento, CA 95819
CC, SC (1996)

Department of Counseling
San Francisco State University
1600 Holloway Avenue
San Francisco, CA 94132
CCOAS, SC, SPC (1994)

Counseling Department
Nichols 220
Sonoma State University
1801 East Cotati Avenue
Rohnert Park, CA 94928
CCOAS, SC (1992)

COLORADO

Counseling Psychology Program
Division of Professional Psychology
McKee Hall 248
University of Northern Colorado
Greeley, CO 80639
☆CC, SC, CE:EdD (1993)

CONNECTICUT

Community and School Counseling
Graduate School of Education and Allied
  Professions
Fairfield University
Fairfield, CT 06430-7524
CCOAS, SC (1994)

☆denotes programs accredited for 2-year period with conditions.

DISTRICT OF COLUMBIA
Department of Human Services
T605 Academic Center
George Washington University
801 22nd Street, N.W.
Washington, D.C. 20052
CCOAS, SC, CE:EdD (1991)

FLORIDA
Department of Counselor Education
1215 Norman Hall
University of Florida
Gainesville, FL 32611
CC, SC, SAC, SAD, CE:PhD/EdD (1996)

GEORGIA
Counseling and Psychological Services
University Plaza
Georgia State University
Atlanta, GA 30303-3083
✩CCOAS, SC, CE:PhD (1991)

Counseling and Human Development
  Services
402 Alderhold Hall
University of Georgia
Athens, GA 30602
CCOAS, SC, SPC, SPD, CE:PhD/EdD
  (1994)

HAWAII
Department of Counselor Education
Room 222, Wist Hall Annex 2
University of Hawaii at Manoa
1776 University Avenue
Honolulu, HI 96822
CCOAS, SC, SPC (1992)

IDAHO
Department of Counselor Education and
  Special Education
Idaho State University
Box 8059
Pocatello, ID 83209
CCOAS/MH, SC, SPC, CE:EdD (1995)

Counseling and Special Education
University of Idaho
Moscow, ID 83843
CCOAS, SC, CE:PhD/EdD (1992)

ILLINOIS
Educational Psychology, Counseling, and
  Special Education
Northern Illinois University
Graham Hall 223
DeKalb, IL 60115-2854
✩CCOAS, SC, SPC, CE:EdD (1991)

Counseling Programs
Department of Educational Psychology
Southern Illinois University
Carbondale, IL 62901-4618
CCOAS, SC, CE:PhD (1995)

Department of Counselor Education and
  College Student Personnel
Western Illinois University
74 Horrabin Hall
Macomb, IL 61455
CCOAS, SC, SPC, SPD (1994)

INDIANA
Department of Counseling Psychology
Teachers College
Room 622
Ball State University
Muncie, IN 47306-0585
✩CCOAS (1991)

Counseling and Development
Engineering Administration Building
Purdue University
West Lafayette, IN 47907
CCOAS, SC, SPC, CE:PhD (1994)

IOWA
Educational Administration and
  Counseling
University of Northern Iowa
508 Education Center
Cedar Falls, IA 50614-0604
✩CC, MHC, SC (1993)

Division of Counselor Education
N338 Lindquist Center
University of Iowa
Iowa City, IA 52242
✩SC, SPC, SPD, SPA, CE:PhD (1991)

KANSAS
Psychology and Counseling Department
Hughes Hall
Pittsburg State University
Pittsburg, KS 66762
CCOAS (1996)

KENTUCKY
Educational Leadership and Counseling
Wells Hall
Murray State University
Murray, KY 42071
☆CCOAS/MH (1991)

LOUISIANA
College of Education
Northeast Louisiana University
700 University Avenue
Monroe, LA 71209-0205
☆CCOAS, SC (1991)

Educational Leadership and Foundations
University of New Orleans
Lakefront
New Orleans, LA 70148
☆CCOAS/MH, SC, CE:PhD/EdD (1992)

MAINE
Department of Human Resource
    Development
400 Bailey Hall
University of Southern Maine
Gorham, ME 04038
SC (1995)

MARYLAND
Pastoral Counseling Department
Loyola College in Maryland
7135 Minstral Way
Columbia, MD 21045
CC (1997)

Counseling and Personnel Services
College of Education
University of Maryland
College Park, MD 20742
CCOAS, CE:EdD (1993)

MICHIGAN
Educational and Counseling Psychology
Bell Hall 160
Andrews University
Berrien Springs, MI 49104-1000
☆CC, SC (1992)

Leadership and Counseling
13 Boone Hall
Eastern Michigan University
Ypsilanti, MI 48197
☆CCOAS (1992)

Counselor Education and Counseling
    Psychology
3102 Sangren Hall
Western Michigan University
Kalamazoo, MI 49008-5195
CCOAS, SC, SPC, SPA, CE:EdD (1991)

MINNESOTA
Counseling and Student Personnel
MSU Box 52
Mankato State University
P.O. Box 8400
Mankato, MN 56002-8400
CCOAS, SC, SPD (1994)
☆CC (1993)

MISSISSIPPI
Department of Counselor Education
P.O. Drawer GE
Mississippi State University
Mississippi State, MS 39762
☆SC (1991)

Counseling Psychology and Counselor
    Education
Southern Station Box 5012
University of Southern Mississippi
Hattiesburg, MS 39406-5012
CCOAS (1992)

NEVADA
Counseling and Educational Psychology
University of Nevada/Las Vegas
4505 Maryland Parkway
Las Vegas, NV 89154-3003
CCOAS (1991)

NEW MEXICO
Counseling and Family Studies
College of Education
University of New Mexico
Albuquerque, NM 87131
CCOAS, SC, CE:PhD/EdD (1991)

NEW YORK
Counseling and Development
Long Island University
C.W. Post Campus
Brookville, NY 11548
CCOAS, SC, SPC, SPD, SPA (1994)

Center for Human Resources
SUNY/Plattsburgh
Plattsburgh, NY 12901
☆CC, SC, SAC (1992)

Department of Counselor Education
Faculty Office Building
SUNY College at Brockport
Brockport, NY 14420
CCOAS/MH, SC, SPC (1994)

NORTH CAROLINA
Department of Counselor Education
520 Poe Hall, Box 7801
North Carolina State University
Raleigh, NC 27695-7801
☆SAC, CE:EdD (1992)

Human Development and Psychology
    Counseling
Appalachian State University
Boone, NC 28608
CCOAS, SC, SPC, SPD, SPA (1991)

Counseling and Psychology
CB 3500, 107 Peabody Hall
UNC/Chapel Hill
Chapel Hill, NC 25799-3500
SC (1993)

Department of Counseling and
    Specialized Educational Development
228 Curry Building
UNC/Greensboro
Greensboro, NC 27412-5001
CCOAS, SC, SPC, CE:EdD (1995)

OHIO
Department of Counselor Education
313C McCracken Hall
Ohio University
Athens, OH 45701
CCOAS, SC, CE:PhD (1984)

Counseling and Special Education
127 Carroll Hall
University of Akron
Akron, OH 44325-5007
CCOAS, SC, CE:PhD (1993)

Department of Counselor and Human
    Education
University of Toledo
2801 West Bancroft Street
Toledo, OH 43606
☆CCOAS, SC (1992)

Department of Human Services
Wright State University
Dayton, OH 45435
☆CCOAS/MH, SC (1991)

Department of Counseling
Youngstown State University
410 Wick Avenue
Youngstown, OH 44555
CCOAS, SC (1992)

OREGON
Department of Counseling
Education Hall 315
Oregon State University/Western Oregon
    State College
Corvallis, OR 97331
CCOAS, SC (1993)

Division of Counseling Psychology
College of Education
University of Oregon
Eugene, OR 97403-1215
☆CCOAS/MH

PENNSYLVANIA
Department of Counseling
Shippensburg University
North Prince Street
Shippensburg, PA 17257
CCOAS, SC, SPD, SPC (1996)

Psychology in Education
5C-01 Forbes Quadrangle
University of Pittsburgh
Pittsburgh, PA 15260
SC (1997)   ☆SPC (1992)

Education and Human Services
Suite 302-308 Falvey Hall
Villanova University
Villanova, PA 19085
CCOAS, SC (1993)

SOUTH CAROLINA
Department of Educational Psychology
Education Building
University of South Carolina/Columbia
Columbia, SC 29208
SC, CE:EdD (1992)

TENNESSEE
Educational and Counseling Psychology
108 Claxton Education Building
University of Tennessee/Knoxville
Knoxville, TN 37996-3400
☆CC, SC, CE:PhD/EdD (1993)

Department of Human Resources
Box 322, Peabody College
Vanderbilt University
Nashville, TN 37203
CCOAS, SC, CE:EdD (1991)

TEXAS
Department of Counselor Education
P.O. Box 13857
University of North Texas
Denton, TX 76203-3857
CCOAS, SC, SPC, SPA, CE:PhD/EdD
   (1995)

VERMONT
Department of Organizational,
   Counseling, and Foundational Studies
405 Waterman Building
University of Vermont
Burlington, VT 05405-0160
☆CC, SC (1992)

VIRGINIA
Department of Psychology
Johnston Hall
James Madison University
Harrisonburg, VA 22807
CC (1996)

Counselor Education Program
169 Ruffner Hall
University of Virginia
Charlottesville, VA 22903
☆CCOAS, SC, SPC, CE:PhD/EdD (1991)

WASHINGTON
Department of Applied Psychology
135 Martin Hall
Eastern Washington University
Cheney, WA 99004
CCOAS (1994)

WEST VIRGINIA
Counseling and Rehabilitation
357 Harris Hall
Marshall University
Huntington, WV 25755-2460
CCOAS, SPC (1993)

WYOMING
Department of Counselor Education
P.O. Box 3374, University Station
University of Wyoming
Laramie, WY 82071
CC, SC, SAC, CE:PhD/EdD (1996)

APPENDIX D

CACREP Accreditation Process

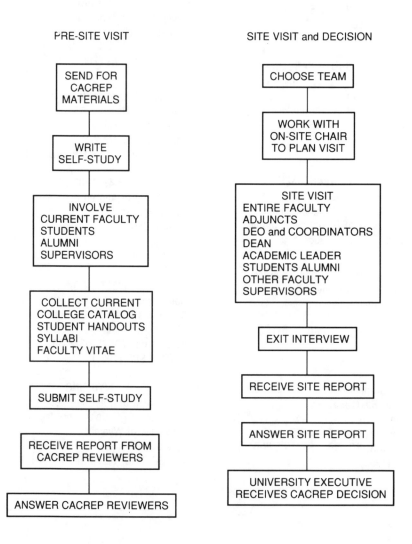

PRE-SITE VISIT

```
SEND FOR
CACREP
MATERIALS
```

```
WRITE
SELF-STUDY
```

```
INVOLVE
CURRENT FACULTY
STUDENTS
ALUMNI
SUPERVISORS
```

```
COLLECT CURRENT
COLLEGE CATALOG
STUDENT HANDOUTS
SYLLABI
FACULTY VITAE
```

```
SUBMIT SELF-STUDY
```

```
RECEIVE REPORT FROM
CACREP REVIEWERS
```

```
ANSWER CACREP REVIEWERS
```

SITE VISIT and DECISION

```
CHOOSE TEAM
```

```
WORK WITH
ON-SITE CHAIR
TO PLAN VISIT
```

```
SITE VISIT
ENTIRE FACULTY
ADJUNCTS
DEO and COORDINATORS
DEAN
ACADEMIC LEADER
STUDENTS ALUMNI
OTHER FACULTY
SUPERVISORS
```

```
EXIT INTERVIEW
```

```
RECEIVE SITE REPORT
```

```
ANSWER SITE REPORT
```

```
UNIVERSITY EXECUTIVE
RECEIVES CACREP DECISION
```

by Michael K. Altekruse, Ed D, Southern Illinois University

NOTES

NOTES

NOTES

NOTES

NOTES

NOTES